VIOLA ▼ BOOK TW

MW01157019

ESSENTIAL ELEMENTS 2000 FOR STRINGS

A COMPREHENSIVE STRING METHOD

MICHAEL ALLEN • ROBERT GILLESPIE • PAMELA TELLEJOHN HAYES

ARRANGEMENTS BY JOHN HIGGINS

Congratulations for successfully completing Book 1 and welcome to Book 2 of *Essential Elements 2000 for Strings!* By now you are well aware of the benefits and joy of playing viola in the orchestra. The techniques you learned in Book 1 will help you reach a more advanced level in Book 2 that will make your musical experiences even more fun and exciting.

You can learn the new skills in the order they occur in Book 2, or you can master a particular skill at the time it most applies to your individual playing needs. Tabs appear on the sides of each page to help you quickly find the section or concept you need to practice.

There will be rewards for your effort! As you spend time learning more challenging material, the mastery of new skills will bring you even more joy in the years to come. Good luck, and best wishes for a lifetime of musical happiness!

ISBN 0-634-05266-7

REVIEW

KEY SIGNATURE

Key of D

TIME SIGNATURE

4/4

NOTES

Whole | Half | Quarter

SLUR

Major Scale

A Major Scale is a series of eight notes that follow a definite pattern of whole steps and half steps. Half steps appear only between scale steps 3–4 and 7–8. Every major scale has the same arrangement of whole steps and half steps.

1. TUNING TRACK

2. D MAJOR SCALE – Round *(When group A reaches ②, group B begins at ①)*

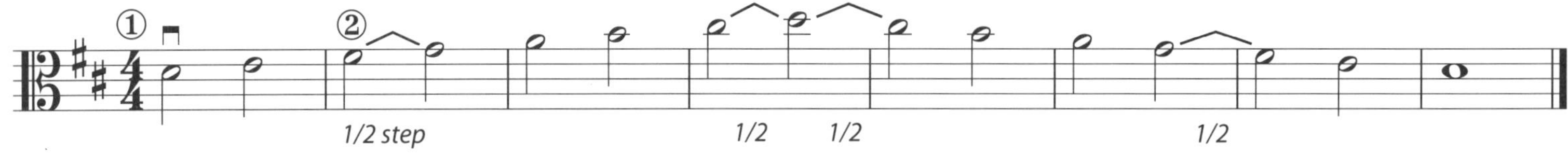

3. D MAJOR ARPEGGIO

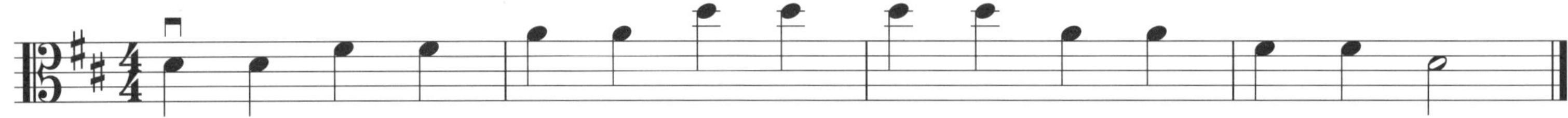

4. D MAJOR MANIA

Legato

Play in a smooth and connected style.

5. THEME FROM LONDON SYMPHONY

Franz J. Haydn (1732–1809)

Morning Song

moderato

Edvard Greig

Forte (f) **Piano** (p) **Bow Lift** (,)

TIME SIGNATURE	NOTES		TIE	TEMPO MARKING	1st & 2nd ENDINGS
	Dotted Half	Eighths			
3/4	𝅗𝅥.	♫		Moderato	1. 2.

6. D MAJOR IN THREES

Dynamics

crescendo (*cresc.*)	<	Gradually increase volume.
decrescendo (*decresc.*)	>	Gradually decrease volume.

7. DYNAMIC CONTRASTS

HISTORY

Norwegian composer **Edvard Grieg** wrote *Peer Gynt Suite* for a play by Henrik Ibsen in 1875, the year before the telephone was invented by Alexander Graham Bell. "Morning" is a melody from *Peer Gynt Suite.* Music used in plays, or in films and television, is called **incidental music**.

8. MORNING (from Peer Gynt)

Moderato

Edvard Grieg (1843–1907)

9. BARCAROLLE

Moderato

Jacques Offenbach (1819–1880)

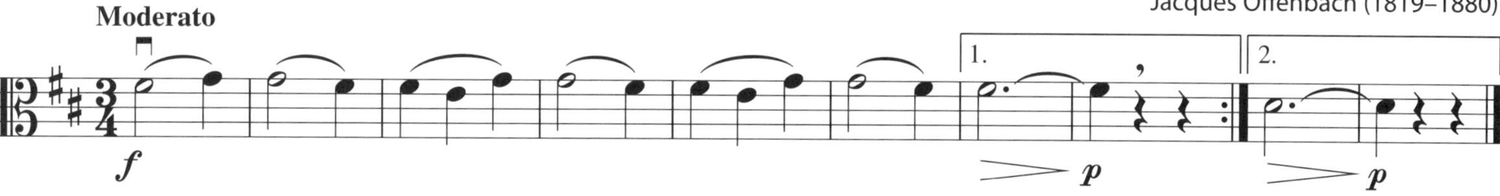

WORKOUTS

Tunneling
Slide your fingers up and down the fingerboard between 2 strings.

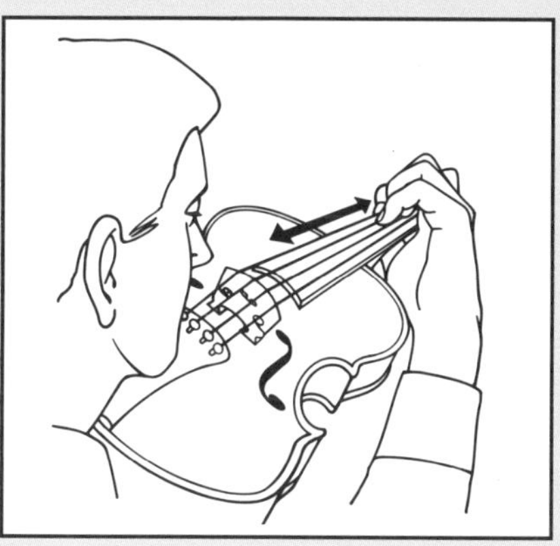

Ridin' The Rails
Slide up and down one string with your fingers.

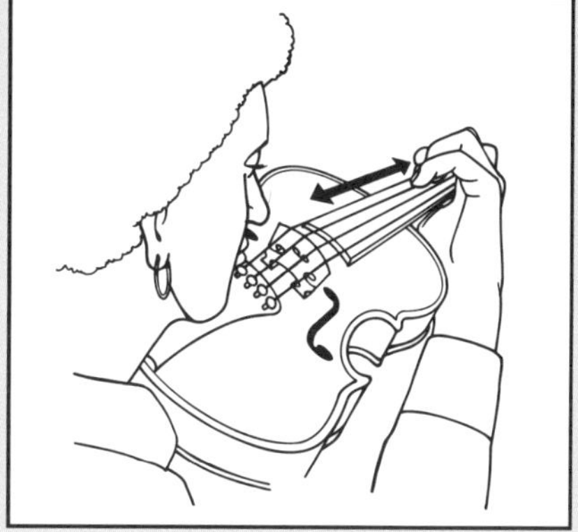

Tappin' And Slidin'
Tap your fingers on any string, slide toward the other end of the fingerboard, and tap again.

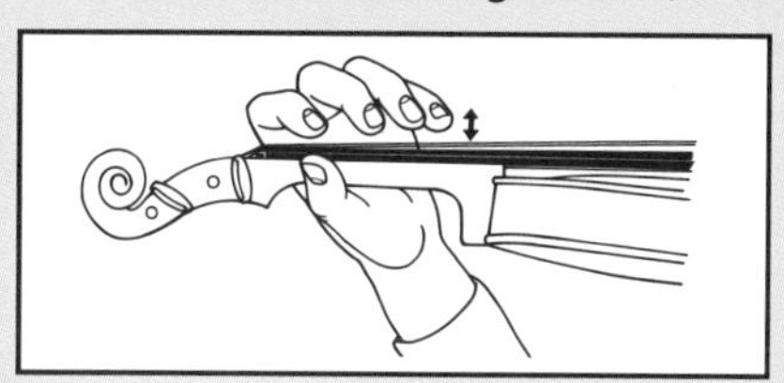

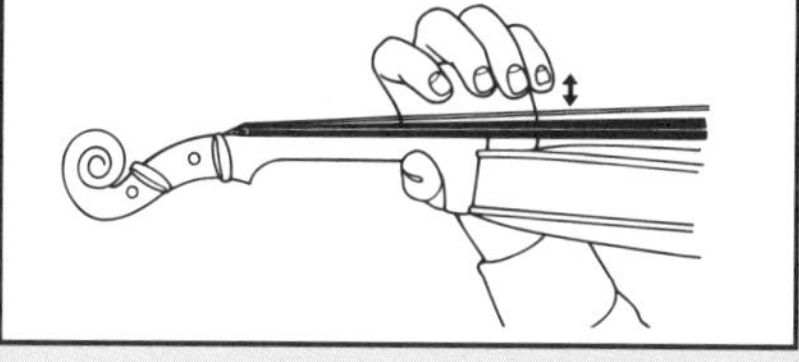

REVIEW

KEY SIGNATURE

Key of G

HOOKED BOWING

TEMPO MARKING

Andante

10. G MAJOR SCALE – Round

11. G MAJOR ARPEGGIO

THEORY

Interval

The distance between two notes is called an interval. Start with "1" on the lower note, and count each line and space between the notes. The number of the higher note is the distance, or name, of the interval.

12. SCALE INTERVALS

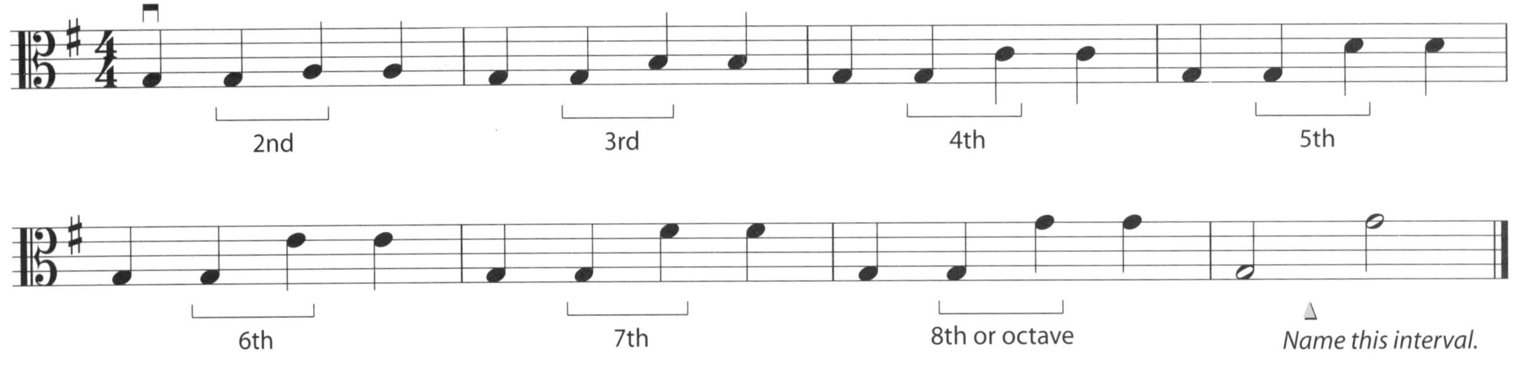

13. CHESTER

William Billings (1746–1800)

Andante

✓ Is your left hand shaped properly?

KEY SIGNATURE

Key of G *(Upper Octave – violin)*

TEMPO MARKING

Allegro

14. G MAJOR SCALE *(Upper Octave – violin)*

15. G MAJOR ARPEGGIO *(Upper Octave – violin)*

Intonation Intonation is how well each note is played in tune.

16. INTONATION ENCOUNTER – Duet

17. THE OUTBACK

KEY SIGNATURE

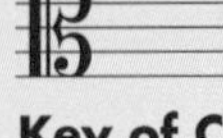

Key of C

TIME SIGNATURE

$\frac{2}{4}$

STACCATO

18. C MAJOR SCALE

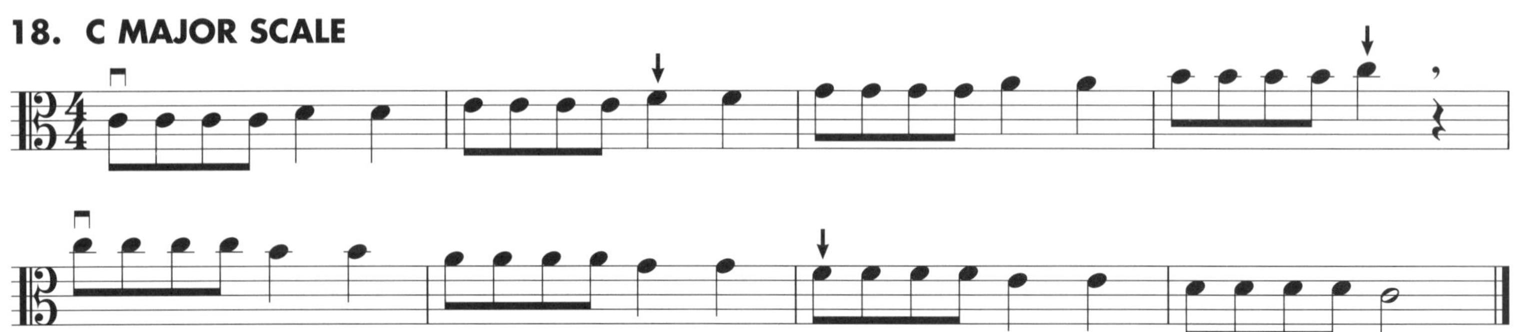

19. C MAJOR ARPEGGIO

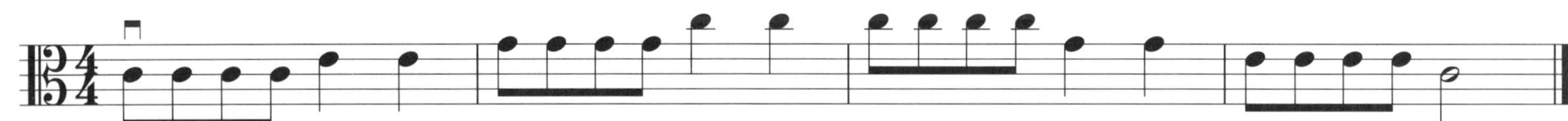

20. C MAJOR DUET

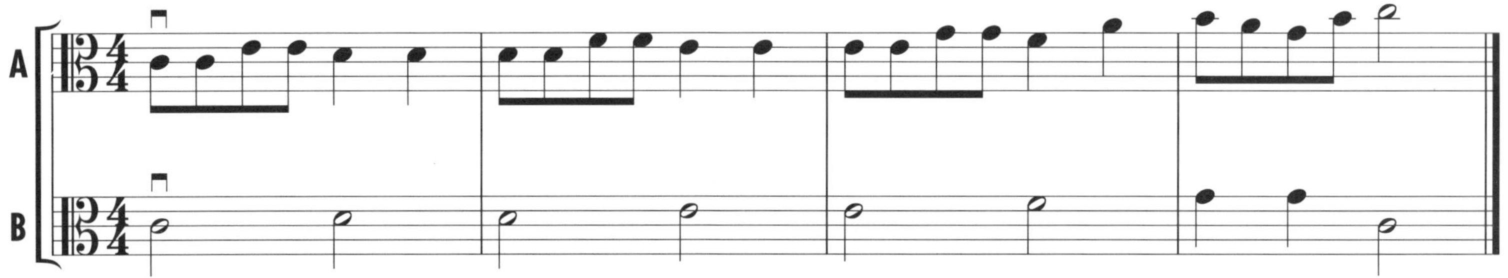

21. BUFFALO GALS

Allegretto ◄ *A lively tempo, faster than **Andante**, but slower than **Allegro**.*

Cool White (John Hodges)

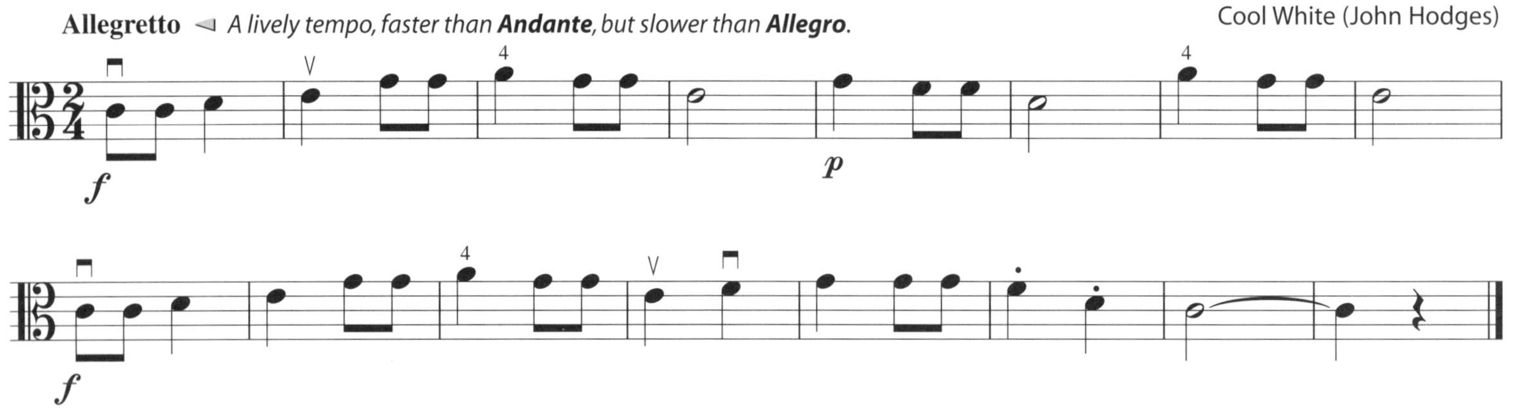

✓ Check your bow hand. Are your fingers curved and is your thumb bent?

KEY SIGNATURE

Key of C *(Lower Octave)*

TIME SIGNATURE

C

TONE PRODUCTION

- place bow between bridge and fingerboard
- bow straight
- proper weight

22. C MAJOR SCALE – Round *(Lower Octave)*

23. C MAJOR ARPEGGIO *(Lower Octave)*

24. C MAJOR MANIA

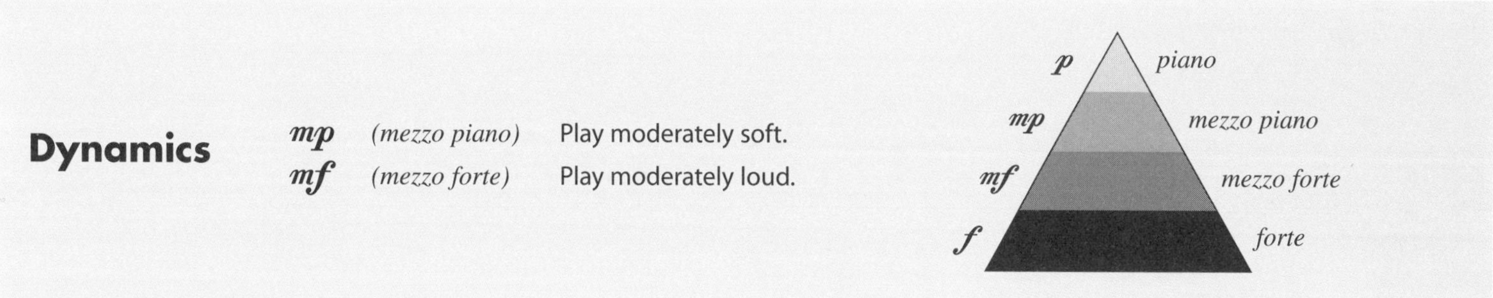

Dynamics

mp *(mezzo piano)* Play moderately soft.
mf *(mezzo forte)* Play moderately loud.

p piano
mp mezzo piano
mf mezzo forte
f forte

25. CROSSROADS

CHANGING BOW SPEED

Change the bow speed according to the length of the note. When you have a longer note value, the bow speed should be slower. If there is a dotted half note on a down bow and a quarter note on an up bow, the speed of the bow must change.

Example:

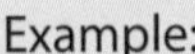

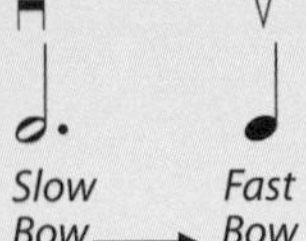

RHYTHMS

26. THE DOT ALWAYS COUNTS

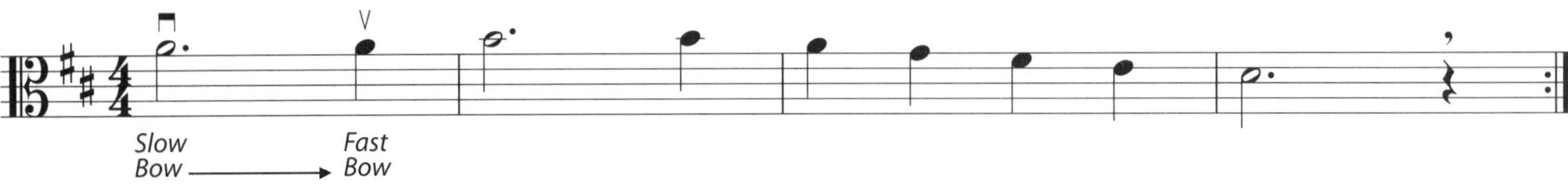

27. ALOUETTE

Allegretto

French Folk Song

28. RIGAUDON

Moderato

Henry Purcell (1659–1695)

29. ESSENTIAL CREATIVITY – OH! SUSANNAH

Make up your own dynamics and write them in the music. Play the line and describe how the dynamics change the sound.

Allegretto

Stephen C. Foster (1826–1864)

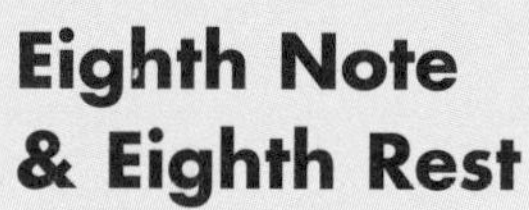

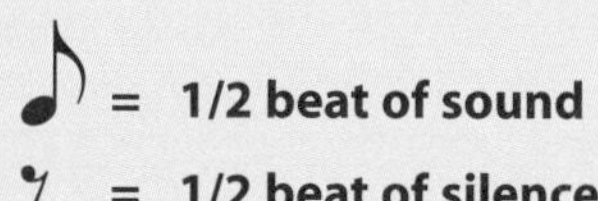

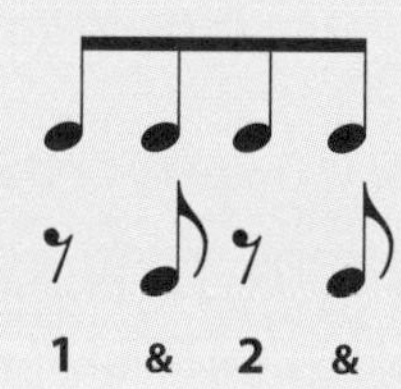

RHYTHMS

30. RHYTHM RAP

Shadow bow and count before playing.

31. EIGHTH NOTES ON THE BEAT

32. SHORT AND SWEET

33. RHYTHM RAP

Shadow bow and count before playing.

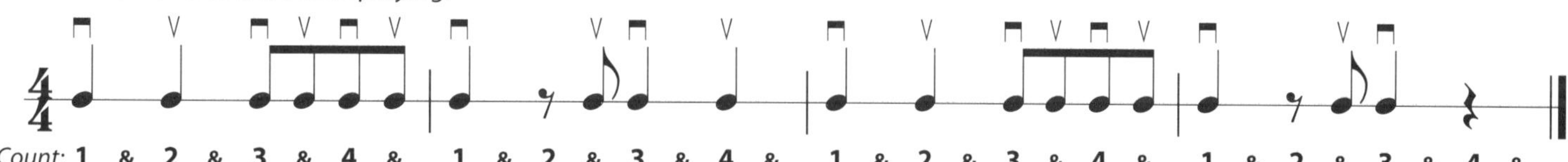

34. EIGHTH NOTES OFF THE BEAT

35. SUNNY DAY

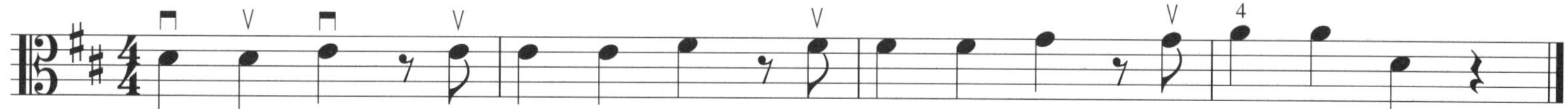

36. ESSENTIAL ELEMENTS QUIZ – JESSE JAMES

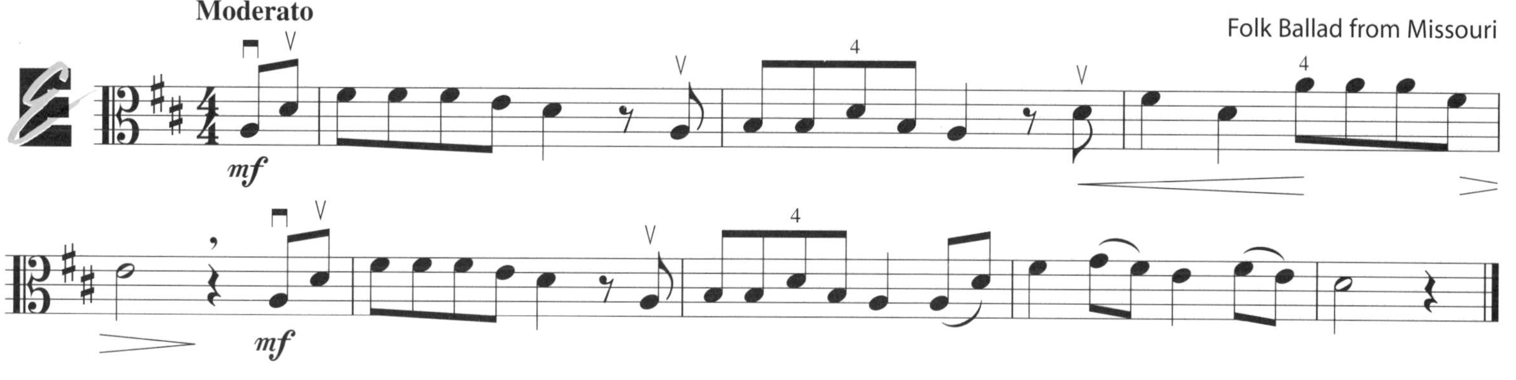

Dotted Quarter & Eighth Notes

A **dot** adds half the value of the quarter note.

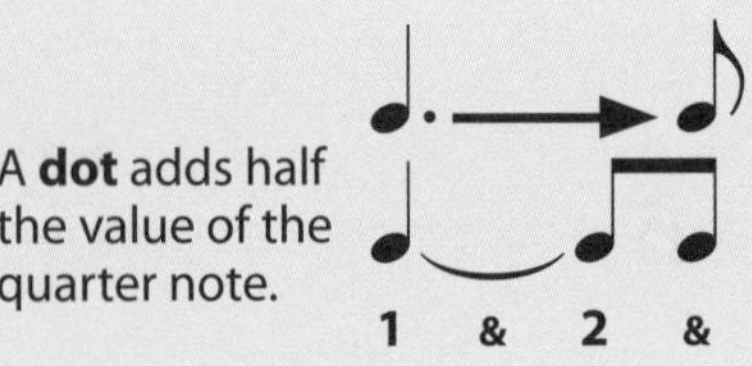

RHYTHMS

37. RHYTHM RAP

Shadow bow and count before playing.

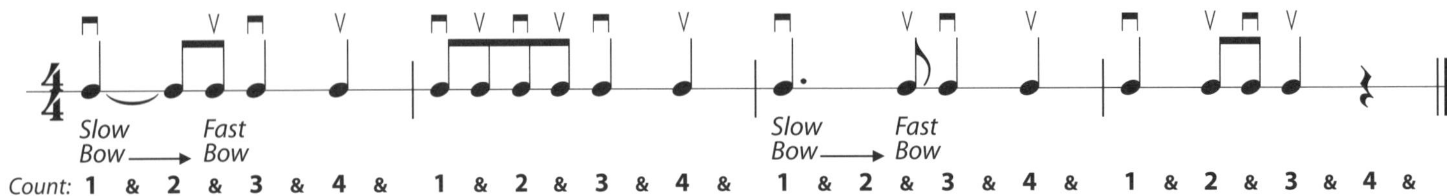

38. THE DOT COUNTS

39. WATCH THE DOT

40. D MAJOR SEQUENCE

41. DOTS ON THE MOVE

Fermata

Hold the note (or rest) longer than normal.

42. D MAJOR BONANZA – Duet

RHYTHMS

43. A CAPITAL SHIP

Moderato

American Folk Song

44. ESSENTIAL CREATIVITY

Create your own rhythms by penciling in a dot and a flag to change any two quarter notes from ♩ ♩ to ♩. ♪

45. HOOKED ON DOTS

Ritardando *ritard.* (or) *rit.* – Gradually slower

46. THEME FROM NEW WORLD SYMPHONY

Lento ◄ *Very slow tempo*

Antonin Dvorák (1841–1904)

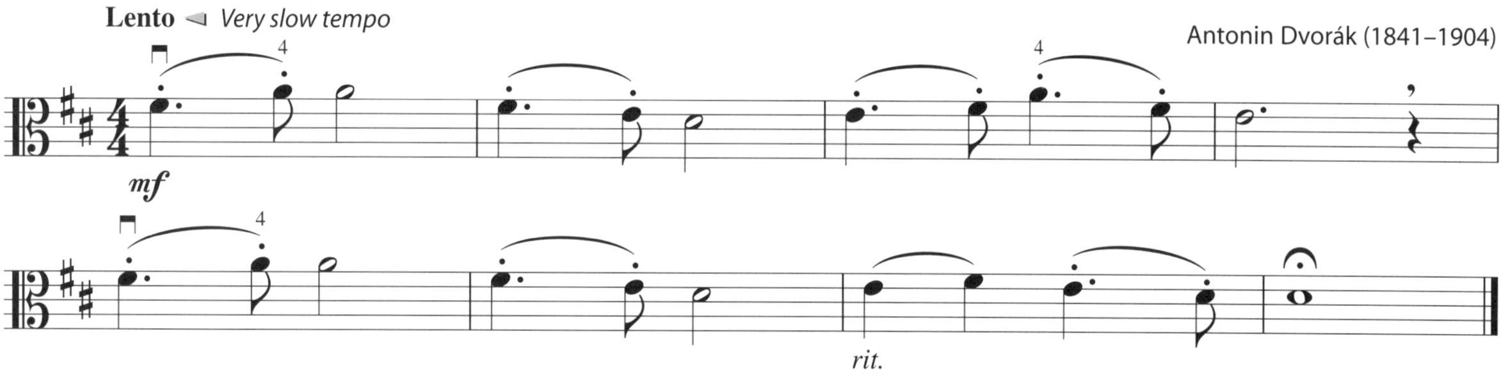

47. ESSENTIAL ELEMENTS QUIZ – RONDEAU

Jean-Joseph Mouret (1682–1738)

Andantino ◄ *A tempo that is slightly quicker than **Andante**.*

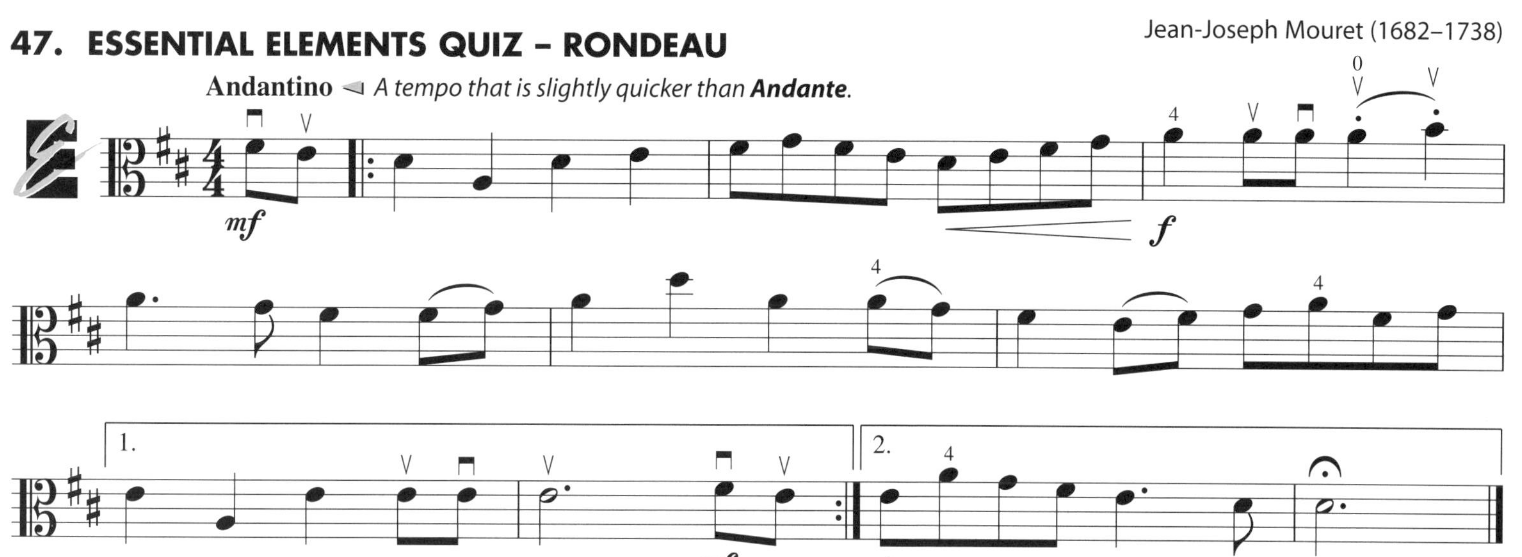

NEW FINGER PATTERN ON THE G STRING

High 3rd Finger

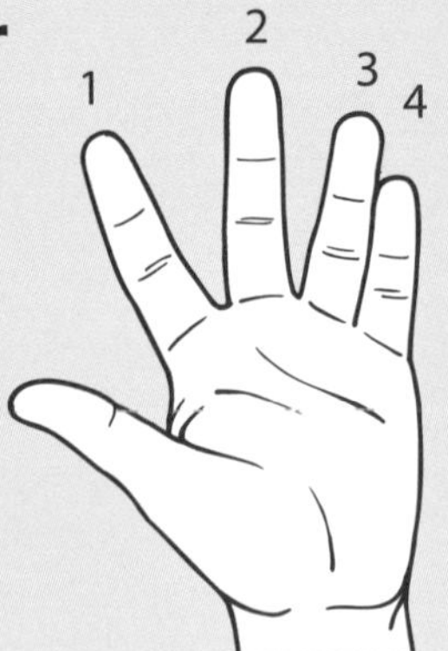

Step 1
Shape your left hand as shown. Be certain your palm faces you. Notice that your 3rd finger lightly touches your 4th finger.

Step 2
Bring your hand to the fingerboard. Your 3rd and 4th fingers touch. There is a space between your 1st and 2nd fingers, and between your 2nd and 3rd fingers.

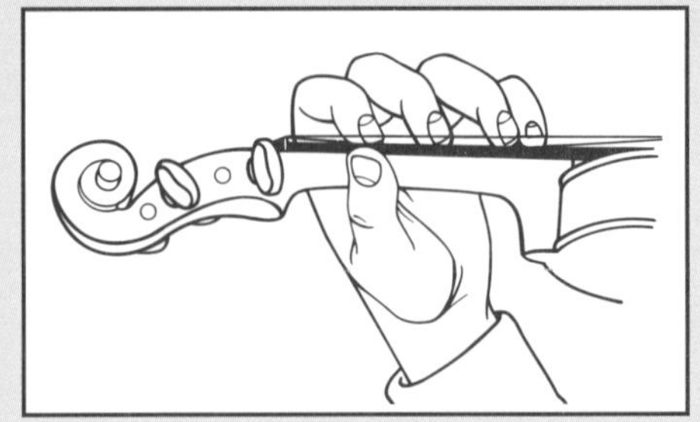

C♯
is played with high 3rd finger on the G string.

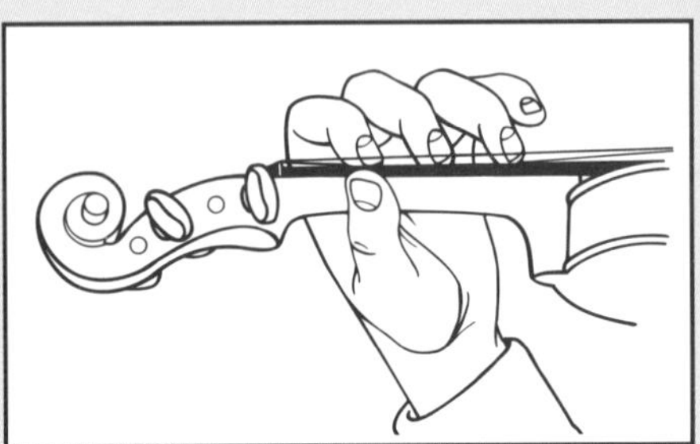

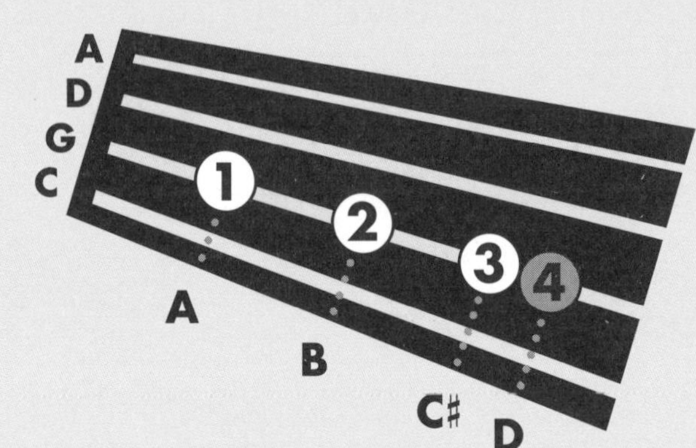

Listening Skills Play what your teacher plays. Listen carefully.

48. LET'S READ "C♯" (C-sharp)

49. STAY SHARP

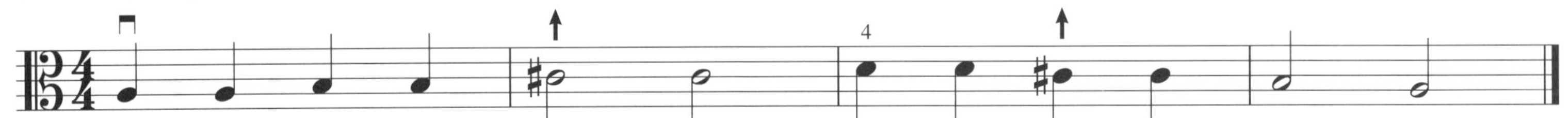

50. AT PIERROT'S DOOR

Andante

French Folk Song

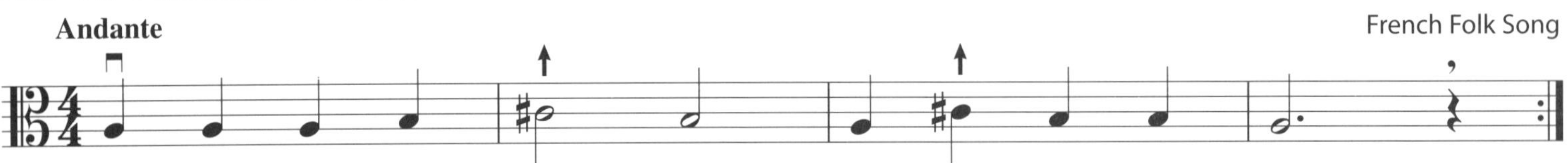

51. HOT CROSS BUNS

Moderato

✓ Were your C♯'s in tune?

NEW FINGER PATTERN ON THE D STRING

High 3rd Finger

Shape your left hand on the D string as shown.

G♯ is played with high 3rd finger on the D string.

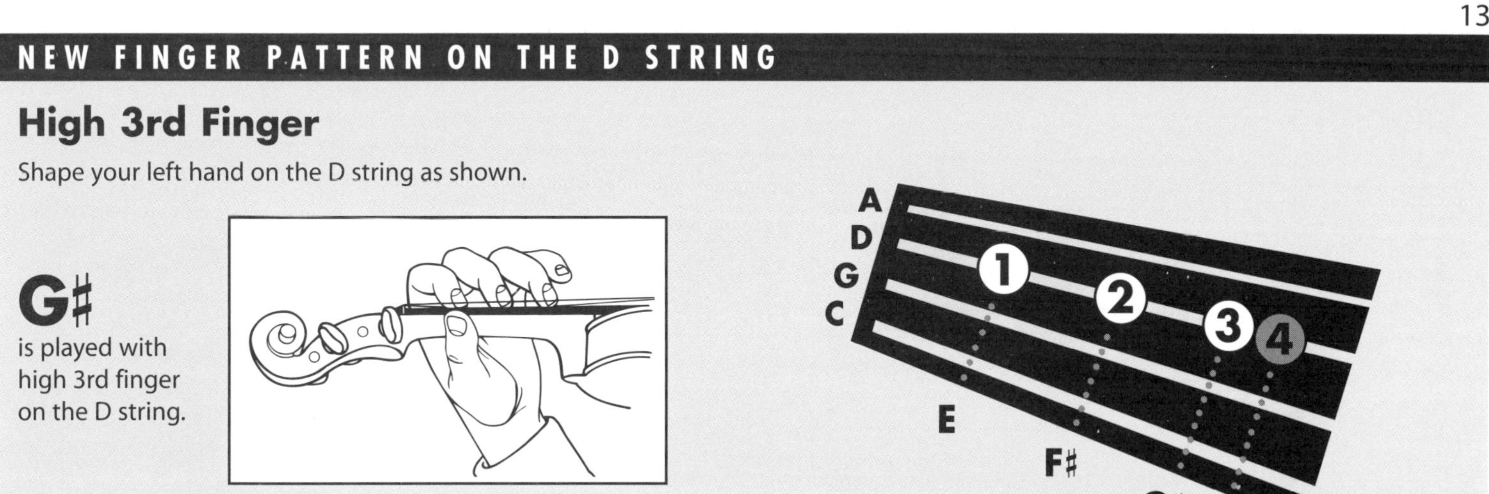

Listening Skills

Play what your teacher plays. Listen carefully.

52. LET'S READ "G♯" (G-sharp)

53. REACHING OUT

54. HIGHER AND HIGHER

Key Signature A MAJOR

Play all F's as F♯ (F-sharp), C's as C♯ (C-sharp), and G's as G♯ (G-sharp).

55. A MAJOR SCALE

56. ESSENTIAL ELEMENTS QUIZ – A SONG FOR ANNE

NEW FINGER PATTERN ON THE C STRING

High 3rd Finger

Shape your left hand on the C string as shown.

F♯ is played with high 3rd finger on the C string.

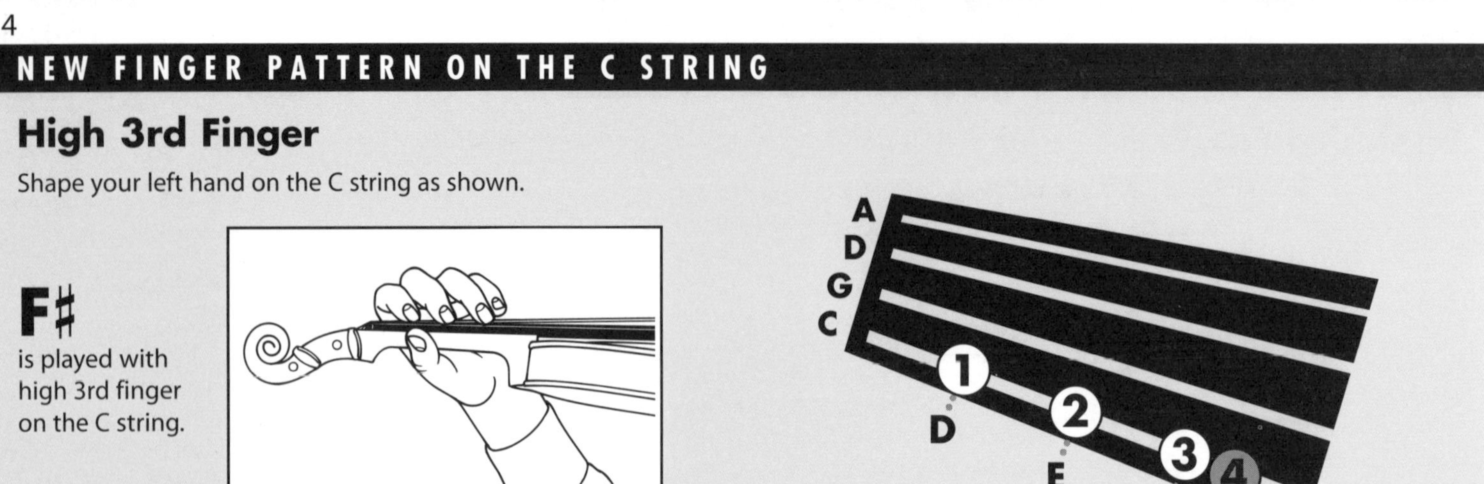

Listening Skills

Play what your teacher plays. Listen carefully.

57. LET'S READ "F♯" (F-sharp)

58. HIGH POINT

59. MAGNIFICENT MONTANA

60. D MAJOR SCALE – Round

HISTORY

In the second half of the 1800s many composers tried to express the spirit of their own country by writing music with a distinct national flavor. Listen to and describe the music of Scandinavian and Spanish composers, and Russian composers such as Borodin, Tchaikovsky, and Rimsky-Korsakov. They often used folk songs and dance rhythms to convey their nationalism.

61. RUSSIAN FOLK TUNE

Special Viola Exercise

While the violins and basses are learning a new note, draw the barlines in the music below. Then write in the counting.

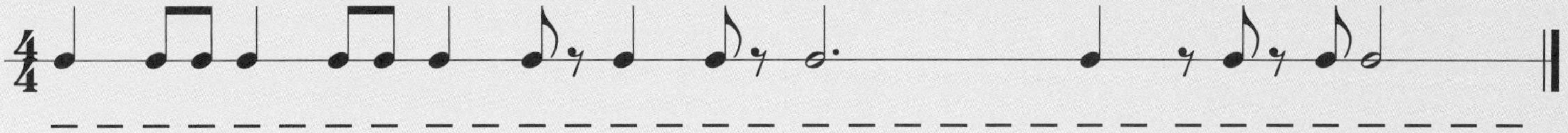

Listening Skills Play what your teacher plays. Listen carefully.

62. LET'S READ "G♯" (G-sharp) – Review

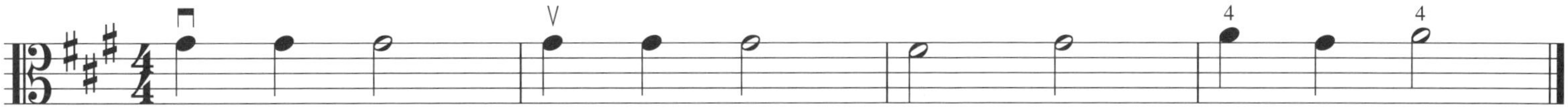

63. A MAJOR SCALE

64. A MAJOR ARPEGGIO

65. THE FIG TREE

Allegretto

Accent Emphasize the note. Add weight or increase the speed at the beginning of the bow stroke.

66. SITKA CITY

Moderato Russian Folk Song

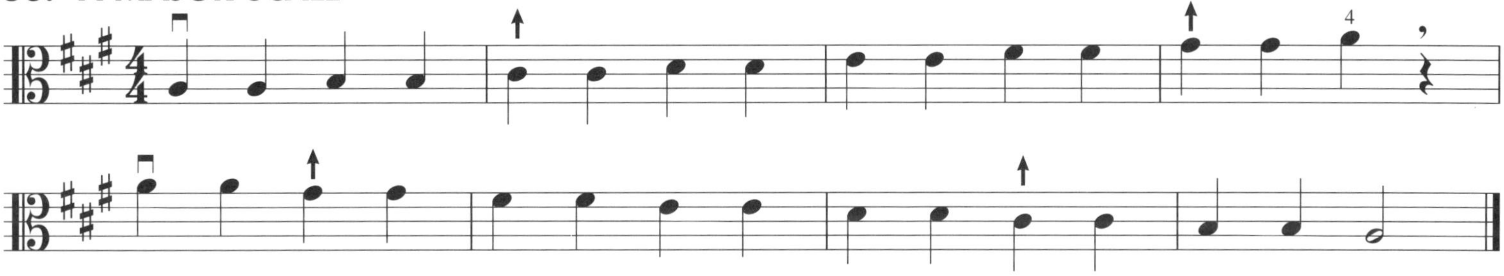

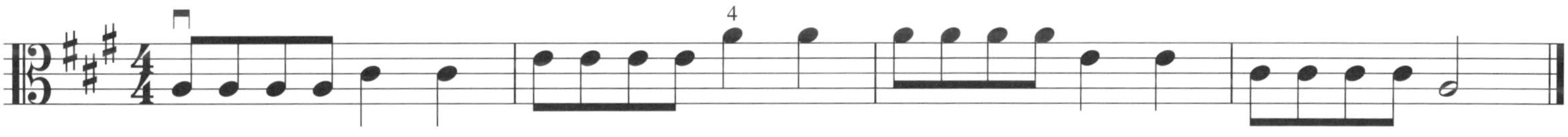

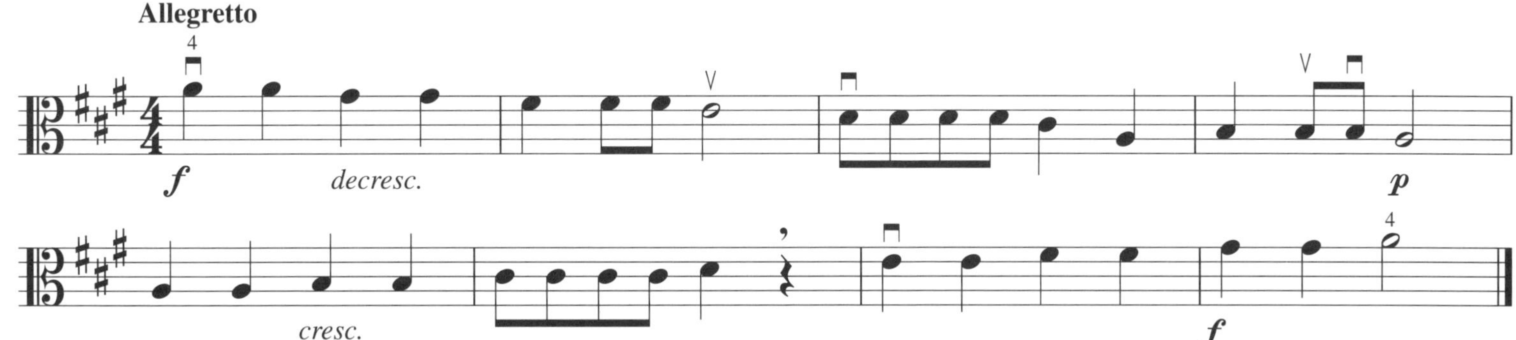

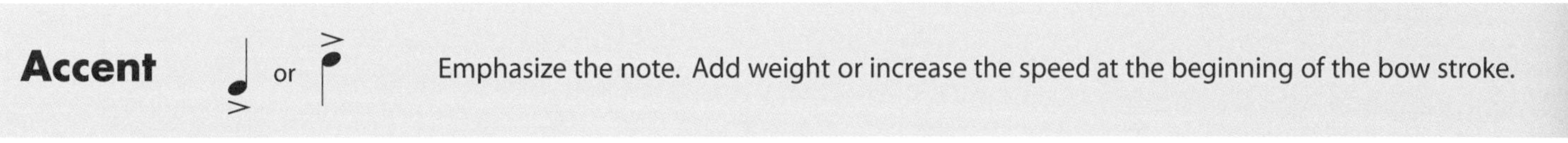

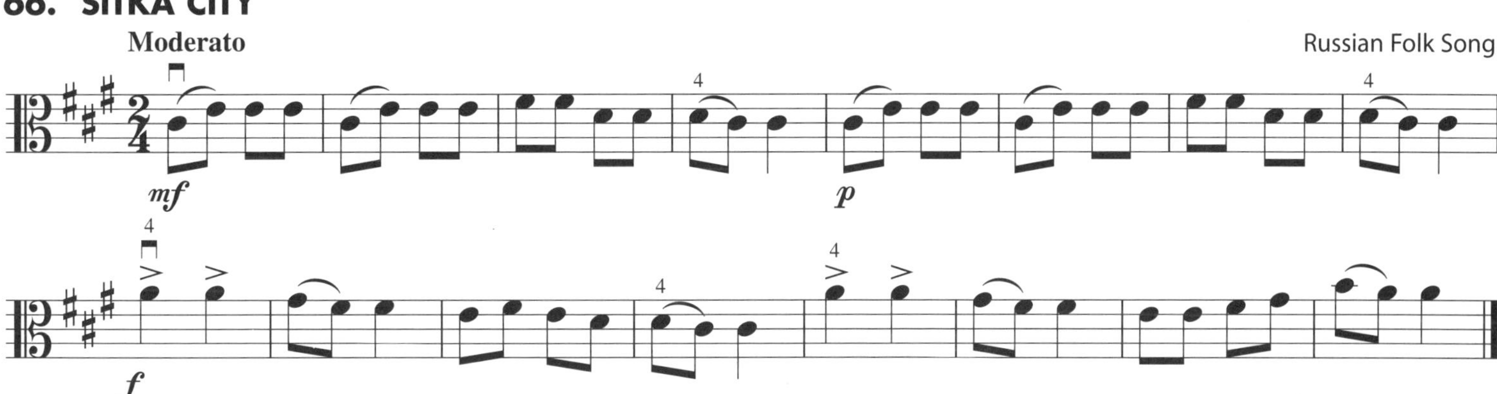

Sixteenth Notes

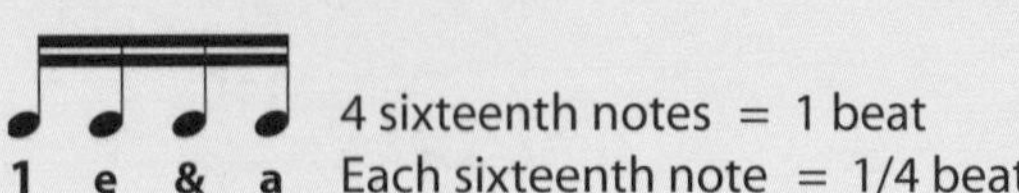

4 sixteenth notes = 1 beat
Each sixteenth note = 1/4 beat

A single sixteenth note has 2 flags on the stem.

RHYTHMS

67. RHYTHM RAP

Shadow bow and count before playing.

68. SIXTEENTH NOTE FANFARE

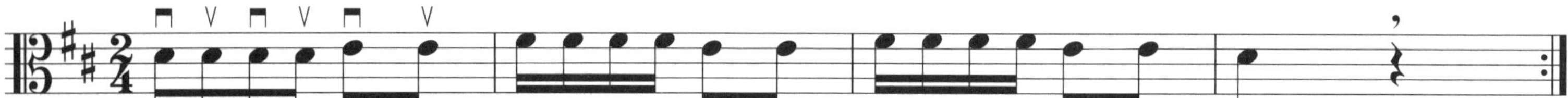

69. TECHNIQUE TRAX

70. DINAH WON'T YOU BLOW YOUR HORN

Allegretto

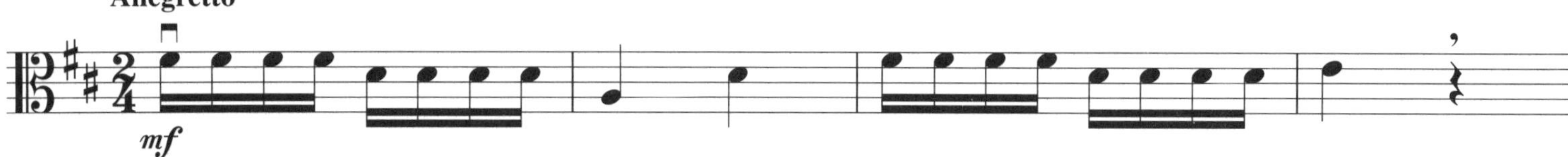

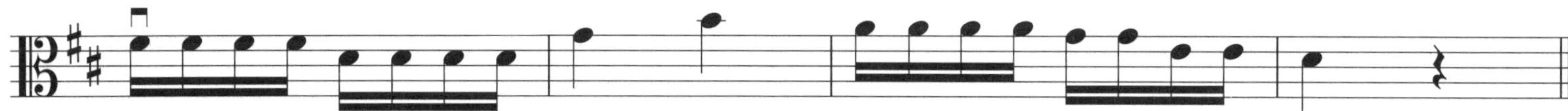

71. MOCKINGBIRD

Moderato

Alice Hawthorne (Septimus Winner) (1827–1902)

72. RHYTHM RAP
Shadow bow and count before playing.
Count: 1 & a 2 & 1 & a 2 & 1 & a 2 & a 1 & 2 &
73. BLUEBERRY PIE
74. TECHNIQUE TRAX
75. RHYTHM RAP
Shadow bow and count before playing.
Count: 1 e & 2 e & 1 & 2 & 1 e & 2 e & 1 & 2 &
76. MARCHING ALONG
77. ON THE MOVE
78. RHYTHM ETUDE – Duet
A
B
79. ESSENTIAL ELEMENTS QUIZ – RHYTHM ROUND-UP
RHYTHMS

80. RHYTHM RAP

Shadow bow and count before playing.

81. TECHNIQUE TRAX

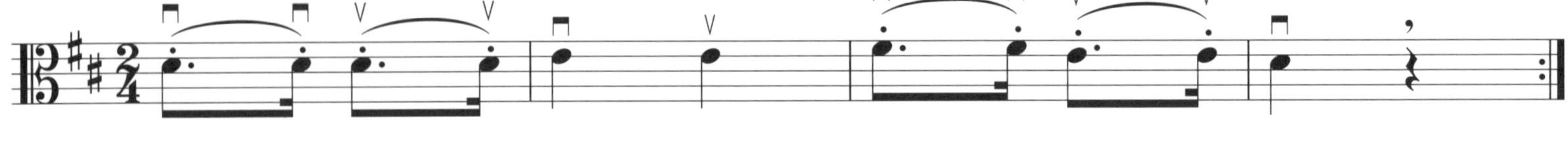

82. HOOKED ON D MAJOR

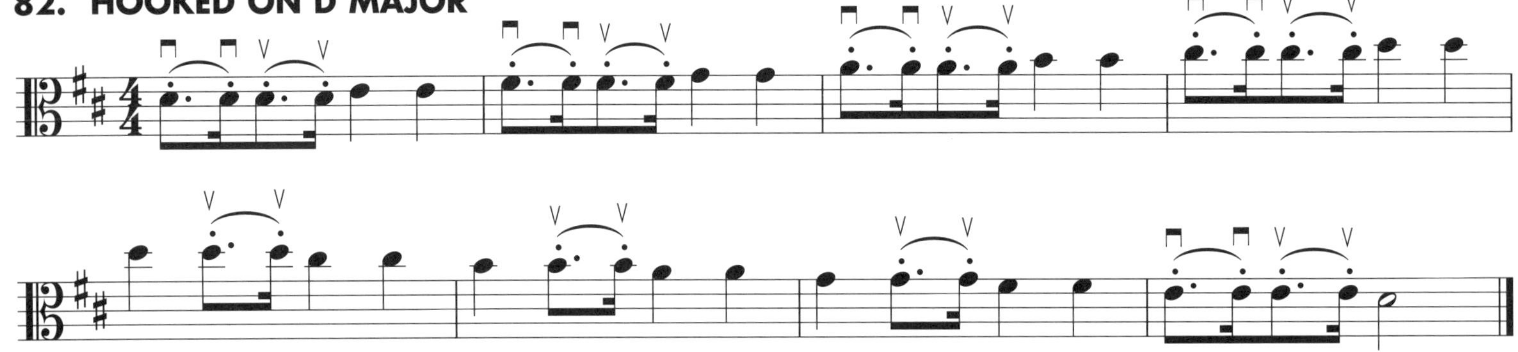

83. THE MOUNTAIN CLIMBER

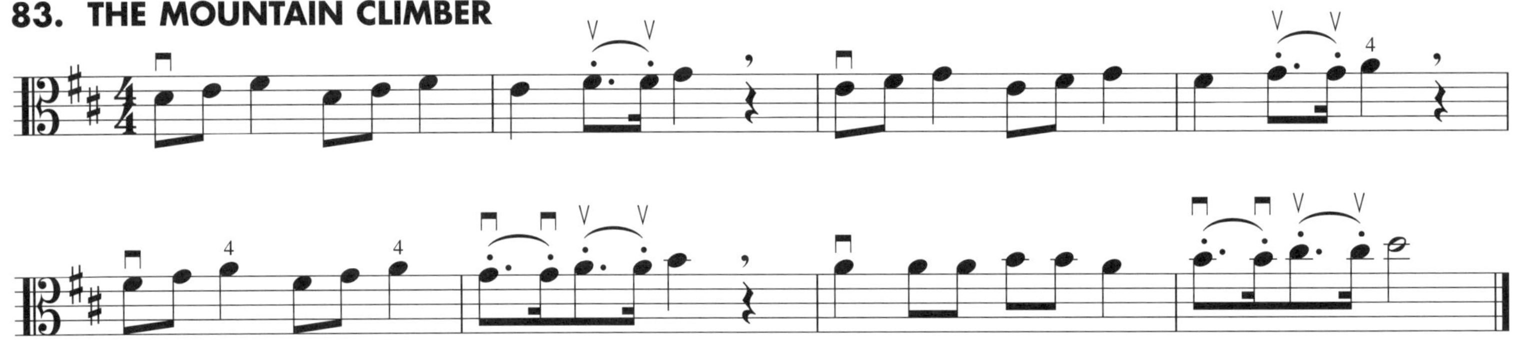

84. KEEP IT SHORT

85. ESSENTIAL CREATIVITY

Write a D Major scale using any of the following rhythms: ♬♬, ♩♫, ♫♩, ♩.♪ *Perform your composition for the class.*

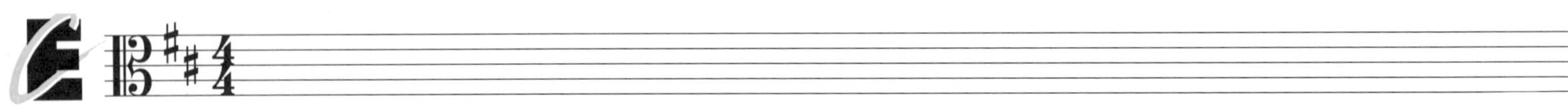

Syncopation

Syncopation occurs when an accent or emphasis is given to a note that is not on a strong beat. This type of "off-beat" feel is common in many popular and classical styles.

86. RHYTHM RAP

Shadow bow and count before playing.

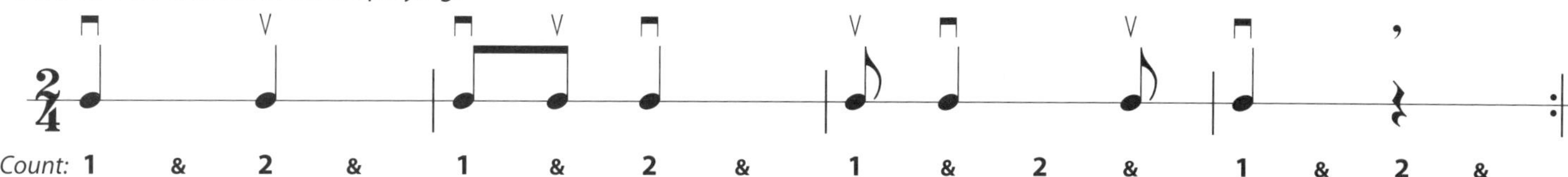

87. SYNCOPATION TIME

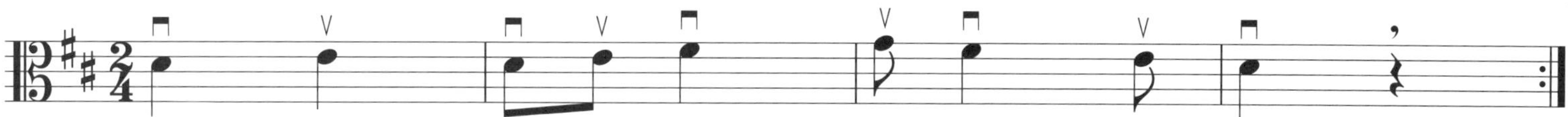

88. MIRROR IMAGE

89. CHILDREN'S SHOES

Black American Spiritual

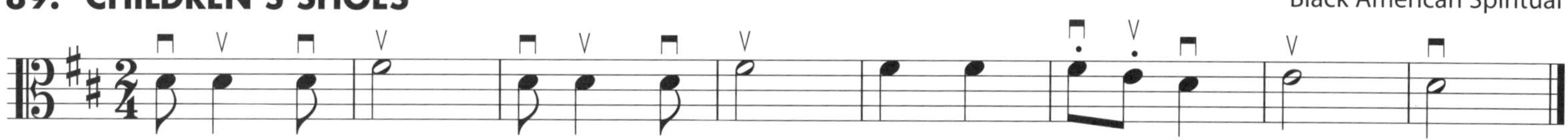

90. HOOKED ON SYNCOPATION

91. ESSENTIAL ELEMENTS QUIZ – TOM DOOLEY

American Folk Song

B♭ (B-FLAT) ON THE G STRING

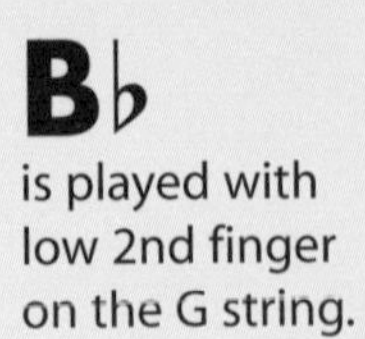

is played with low 2nd finger on the G string.

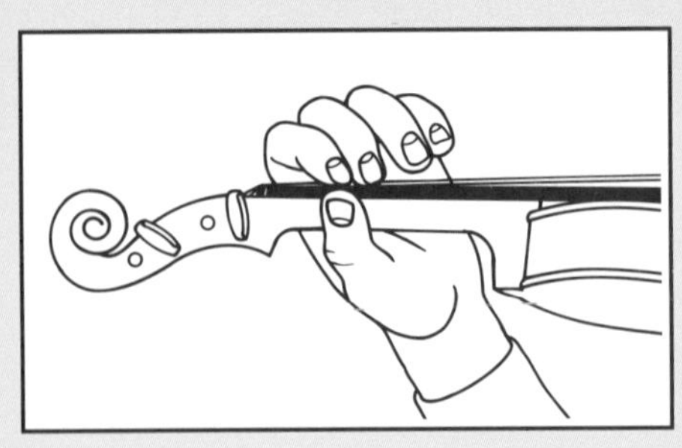

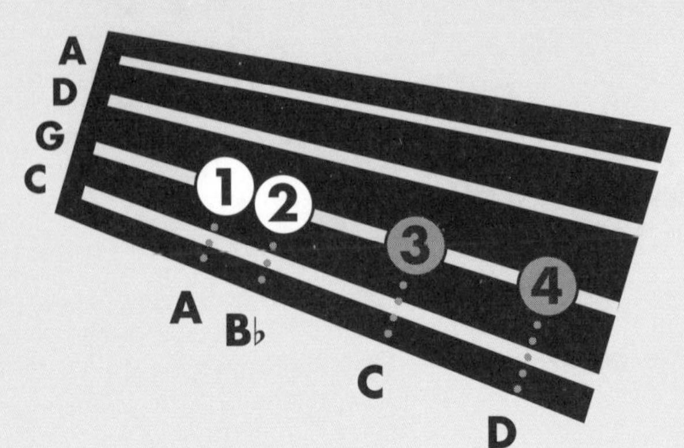

Listening Skills Play what your teacher plays. Listen carefully.

92. LET'S READ "B♭" (B-flat)

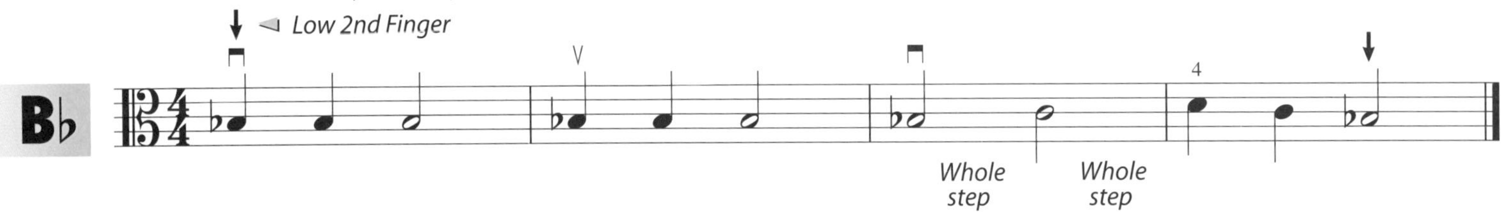

93. ROLLING ALONG

94. MATCHING OCTAVES

Team Work

Great musicians give encouragement to their fellow performers. Violin and bass players will now learn a new challenging skill. The success of your orchestra depends on everyone's talent and patience. Play your best as members of these sections advance their musical technique.

Special Viola Exercise

Draw a note next to each printed note that will match the interval number shown. The note you draw can be higher or lower than the printed note. The first one is done for you.

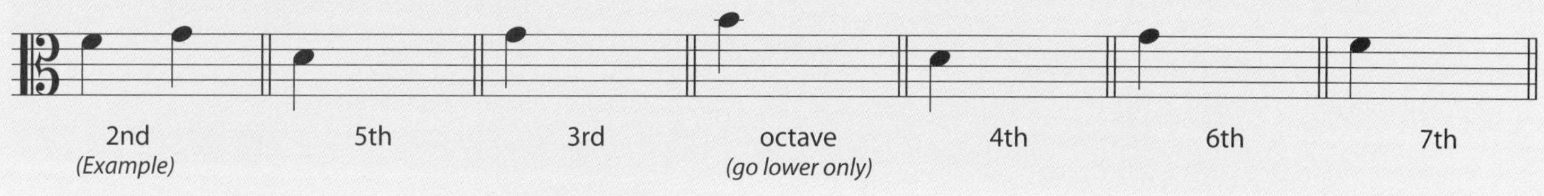

95. LET'S READ "F" (F-natural) – Review

96. TECHNIQUE TRAX

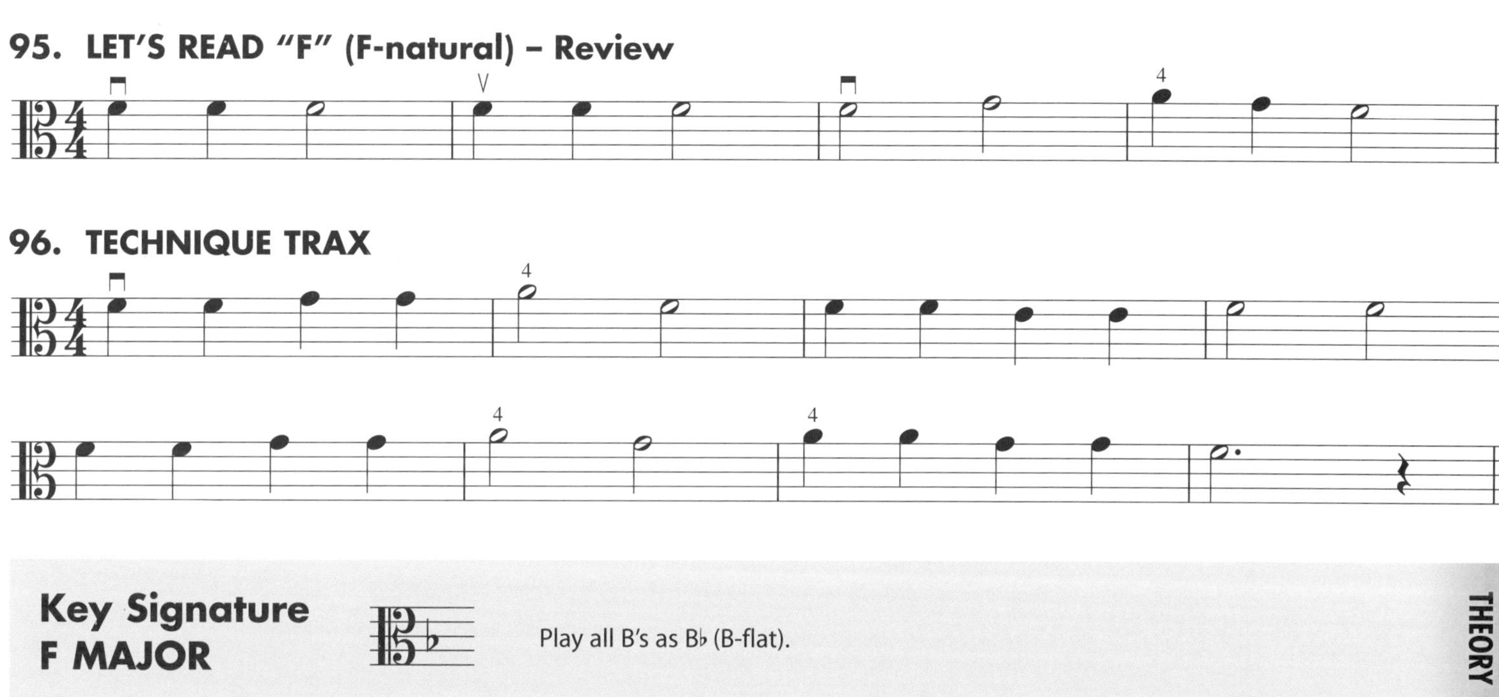

Key Signature F MAJOR

Play all B's as B♭ (B-flat).

THEORY

97. F MAJOR SCALE

A **Concerto** is a composition in several movements for solo instrument and orchestra. Exercise 98 is the theme from the first movement of the *Concerto for Violin and Orchestra* by **Ludwig van Beethoven**, composed while author William Wordsworth was writing his poem *I Wandered Lonely as a Cloud*. A special feature of the concerto is the *cadenza*, which was improvised, or made up, by the soloist during a concert. Improvising and creating your own music is great fun. Try it if you have not already.

HISTORY

98. THEME FROM VIOLIN CONCERTO

Andante — Ludwig van Beethoven (1770–1827)

NEW FINGER PATTERN ON THE D AND A STRINGS

Low 1st Finger

Step 1
Shape your left hand as shown. Be certain your palm faces you. Notice that there is a space between all four fingers.

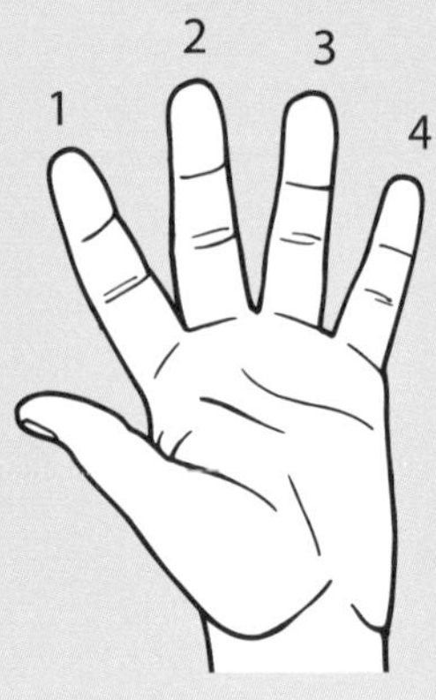

Step 2
Bring your hand to the fingerboard. There is a space between your 1st and 2nd fingers, between your 2nd and 3rd fingers, and between your 3rd and 4th fingers.

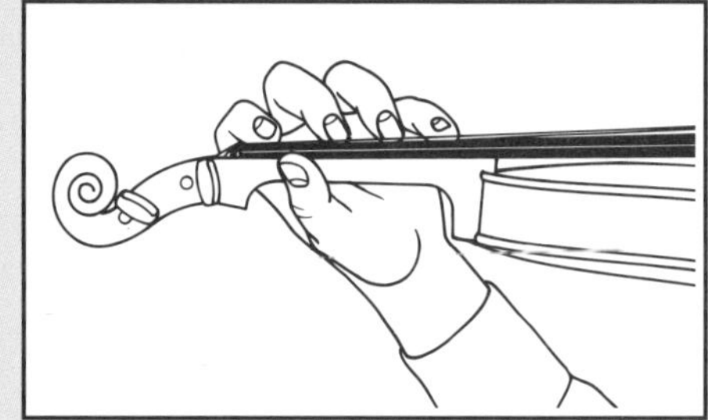

E♭ is played with low 1st finger on the D string.

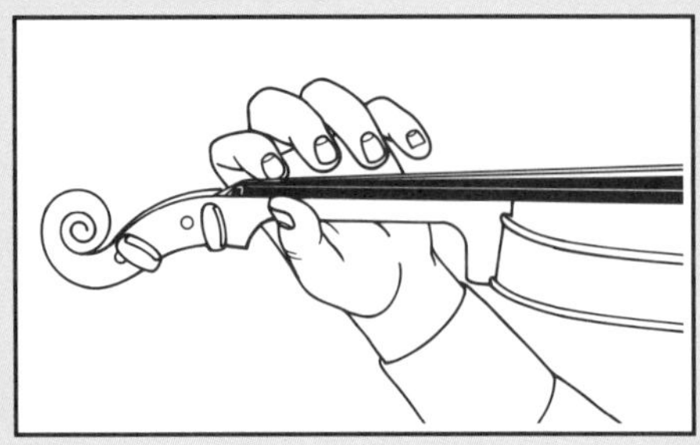

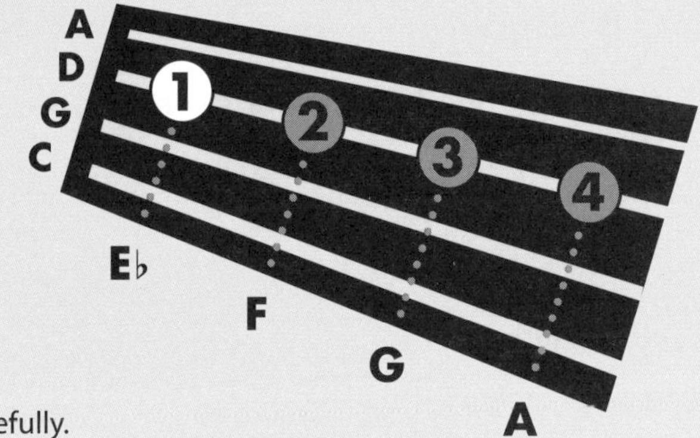

Listening Skills Play what your teacher plays. Listen carefully.

99. LET'S READ "E♭" (E-flat)

100. HOT CROSS BUNS

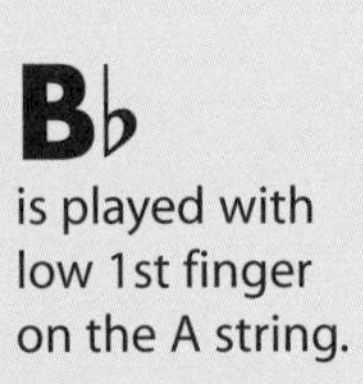

B♭ is played with low 1st finger on the A string.

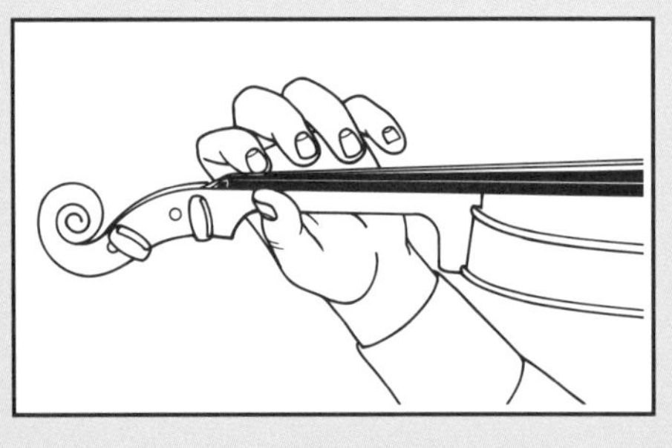

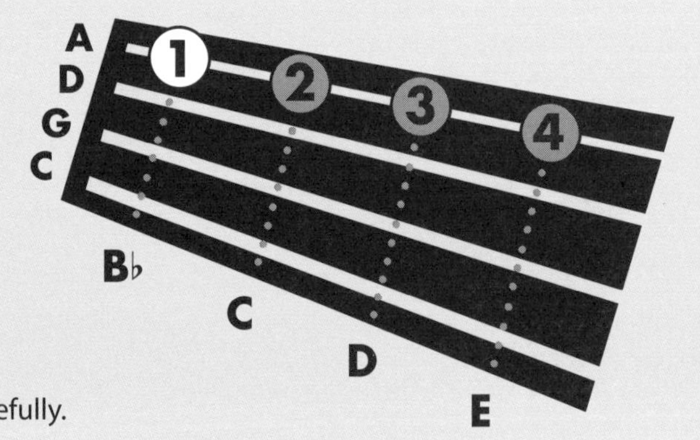

Listening Skills Play what your teacher plays. Listen carefully.

101. LET'S READ "B♭" (B-flat)

102. VIKING WAY

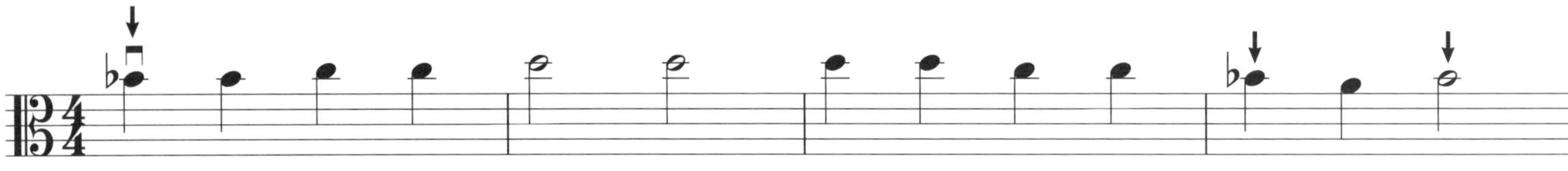

103. HIKING ALONG

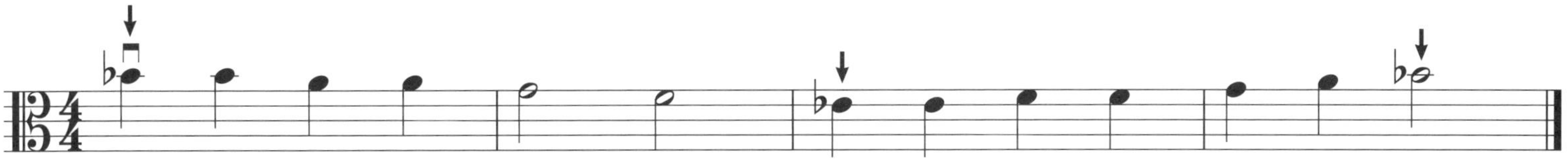

Key Signature B♭ MAJOR

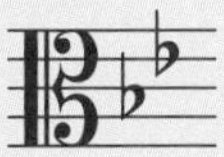

THEORY

Play all B's as B♭ (B-flat) and all E's as E♭ (E-flat).

104. B♭ MAJOR SCALE

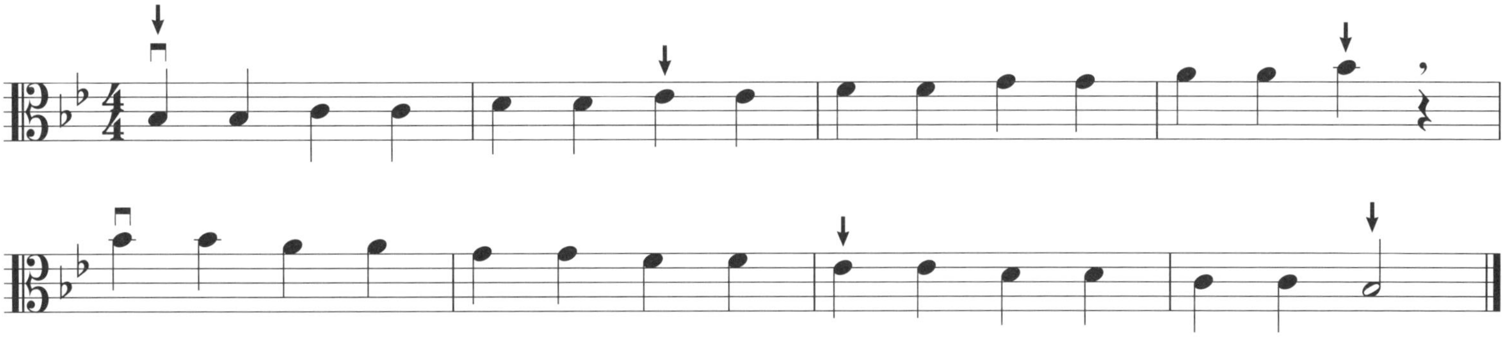

105. SLOVAKIAN FOLK SONG

Allegro

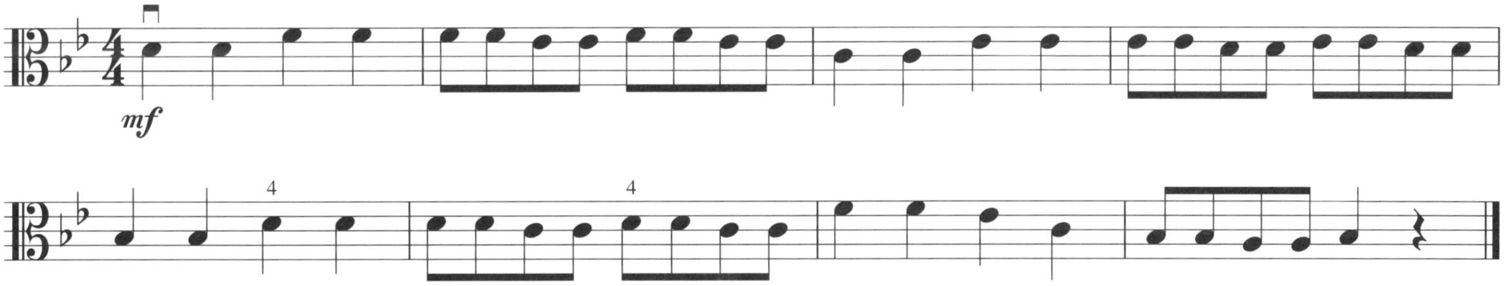

mf

106. CAVALIER COUNTRY

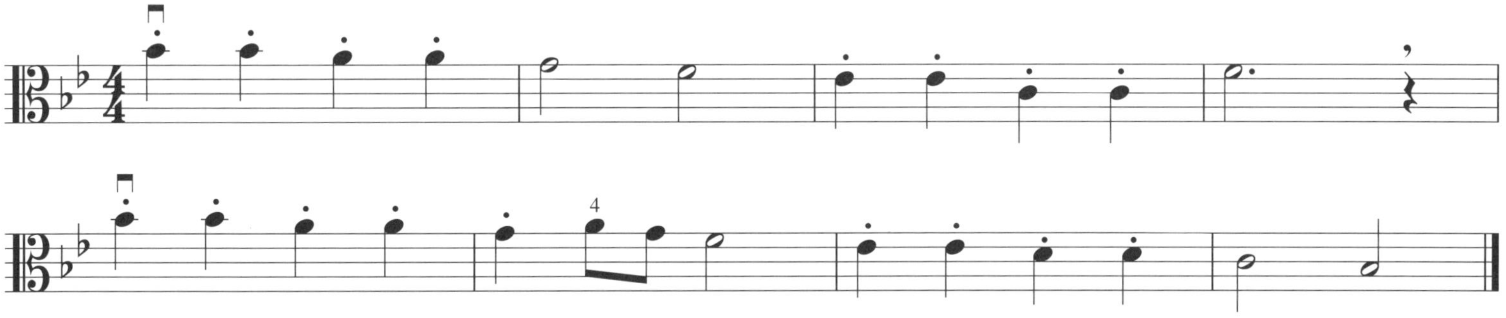

107. ESSENTIAL ELEMENTS QUIZ – AYN KAYLOKAYNU

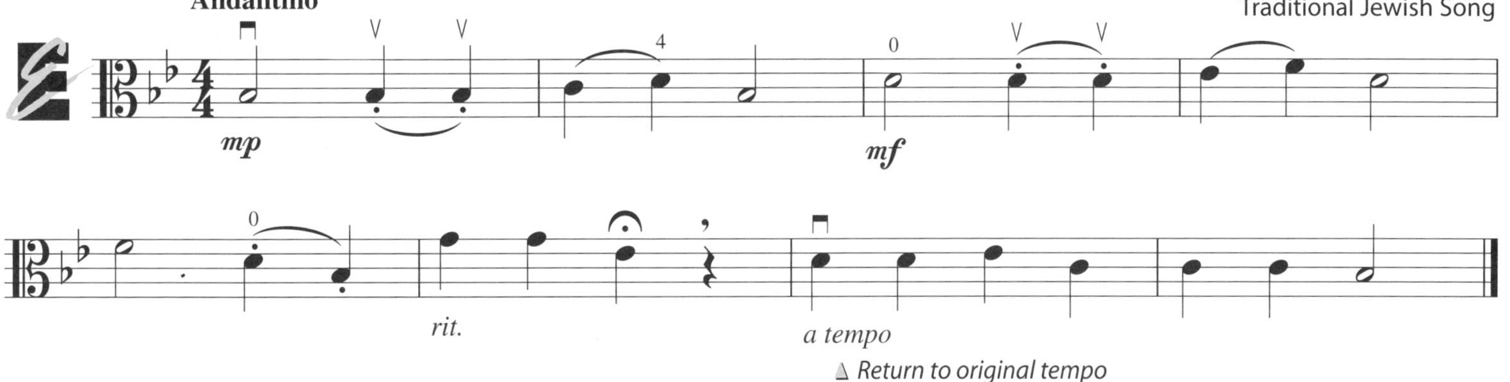

NEW FINGER PATTERN ON THE A STRING

Low 4th Finger

Step 1 Shape your left hand as shown. Be certain your palm faces you. Notice that your 3rd and 4th fingers lightly touch..

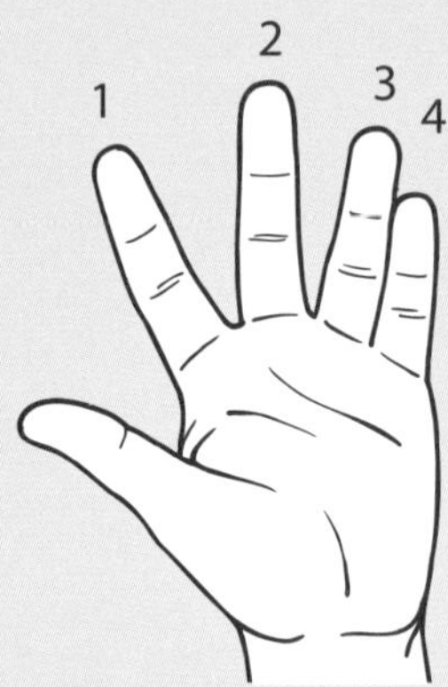

Step 2 Bring your hand to the fingerboard. Your 3rd and 4th fingers touch. There is a space between your 1st and 2nd fingers, and between your 2nd and 3rd fingers.

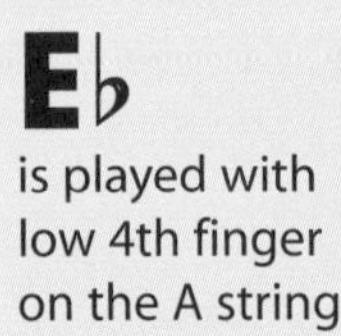

E♭ is played with low 4th finger on the A string.

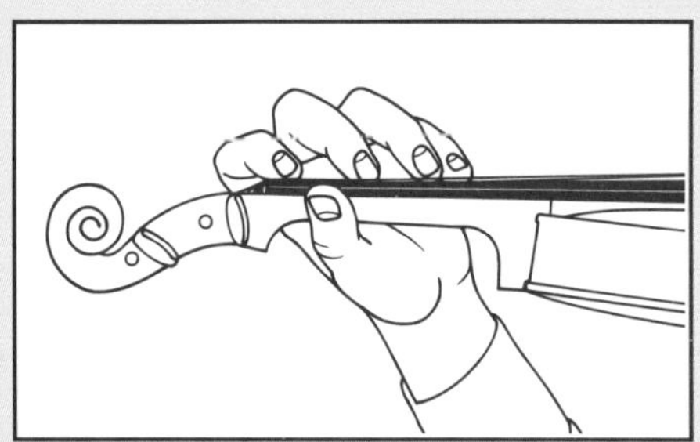

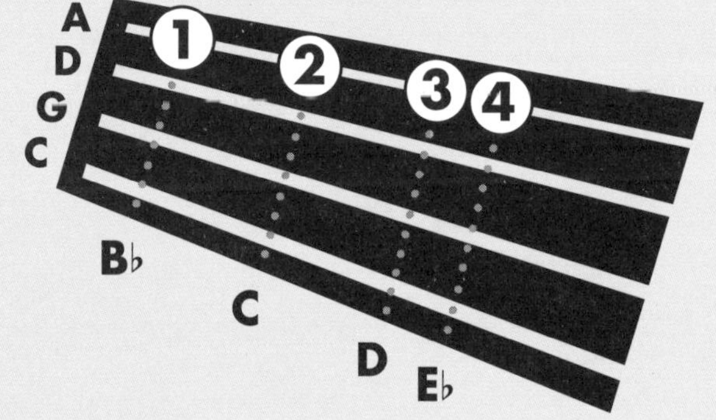

Listening Skills

Play what your teacher plays. Listen carefully.

108. LET'S READ "E♭" (E-flat)

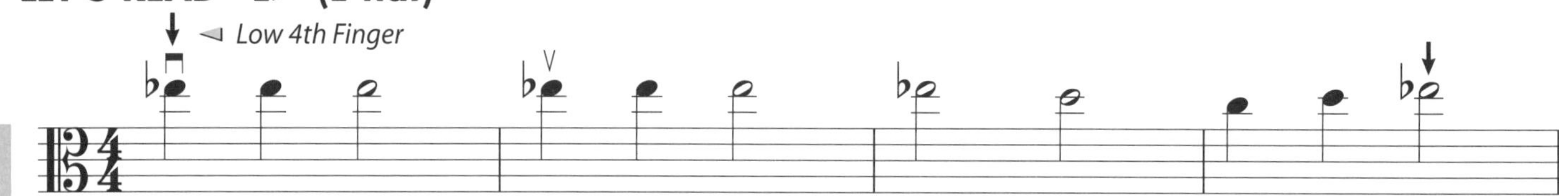

109. TECHNIQUE TRAX

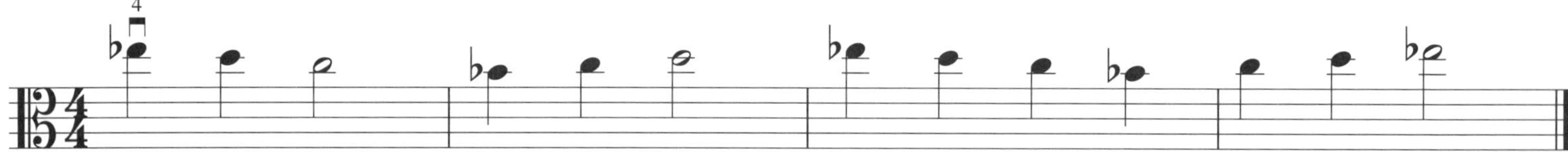

110. LET'S READ "B♭" (B-flat) – Review

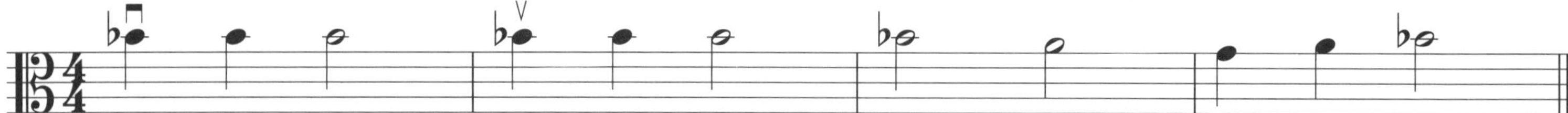

111. TECHNIQUE BUILDER

112. B♭ MAJOR SCALE

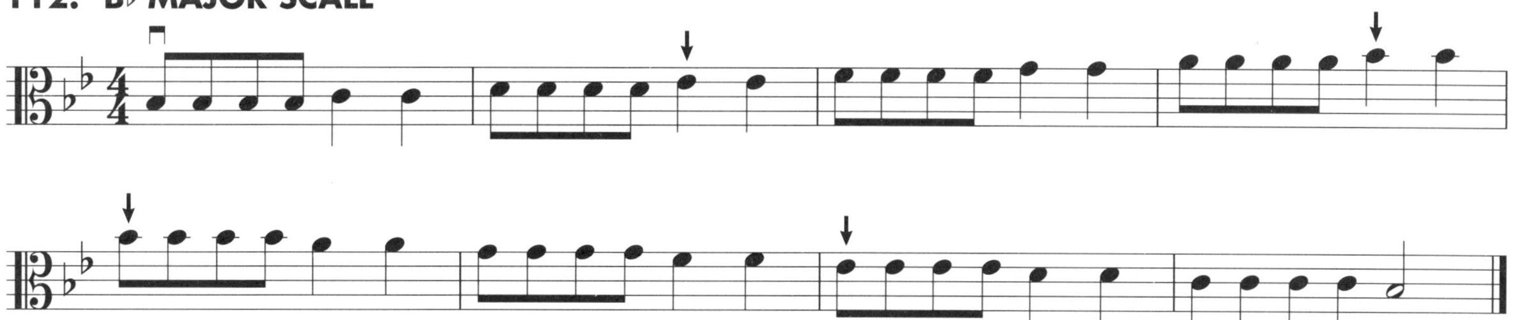

113. THE MOUNTAIN DEER CHASE

114. ESSENTIAL CREATIVITY – RAKES OF MALLOW

Music can be created and arranged by changing rhythms and notes to an existing example. Create your own arrangement of *Rakes of Mallow* by changing the rhythms and melodic phrases. Perform your arrangement for others.

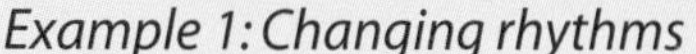

Example 1: Changing rhythms

Example 2: Changing melodic phrases

THEORY

6/8 Time Signature

6/8 = **6 beats** per measure = **Eighth** note gets one beat

♪ = 1 beat ♩ = 2 beats ♩. = 3 beats 𝅗𝅥. = 6 beats

6/8 time is usually played with a slight emphasis on the **1st** and **4th** beats of each measure. This divides the measure into 2 groups of 3 beats each.

6/8 RHYTHMS

115. RHYTHM RAP

Shadow bow and count before playing.

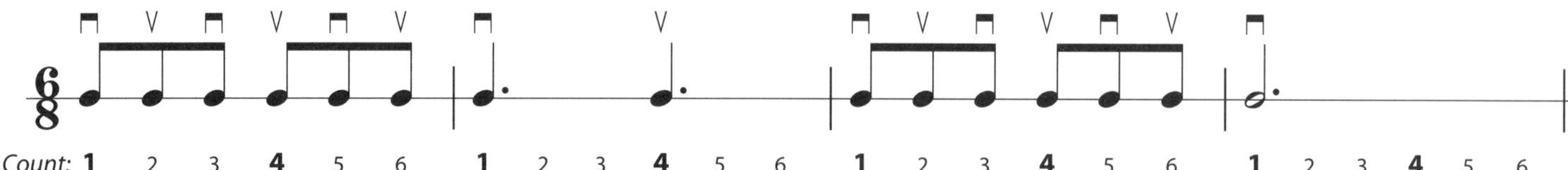

116. LAZY DAY

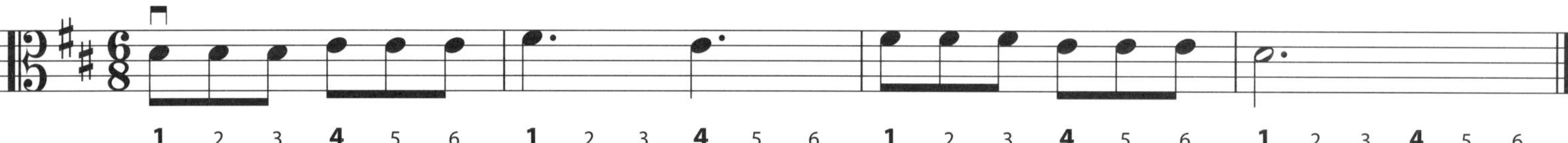

117. HOOKED ON 6/8

THEORY

Musical Form

A round is a **musical form** where performers play or sing the same melody, entering at different times. This is called counterpoint, a type of harmony. Try memorizing this round and performing it with a friend.

118. ROW, ROW, ROW YOUR BOAT – Round

American Folk Round

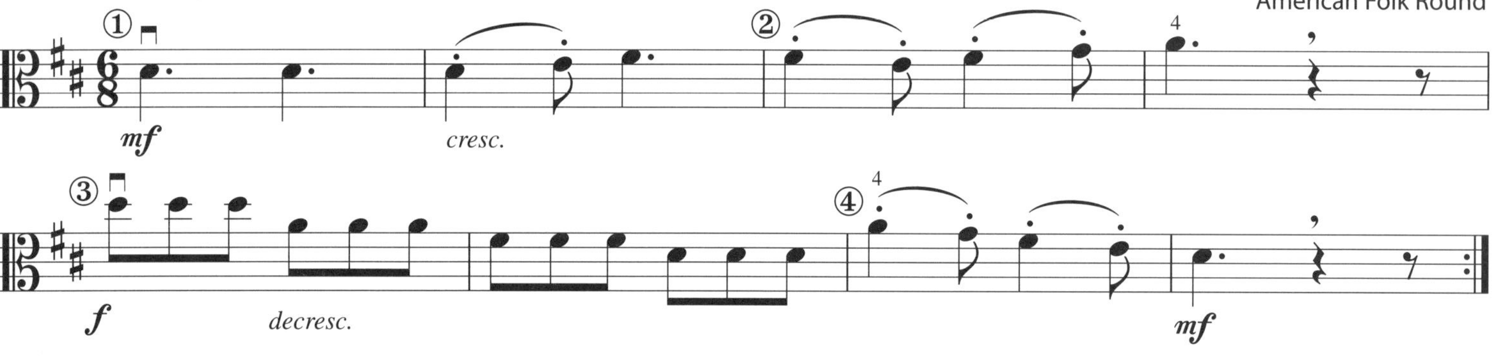

119. SLURRING IN 6/8 TIME

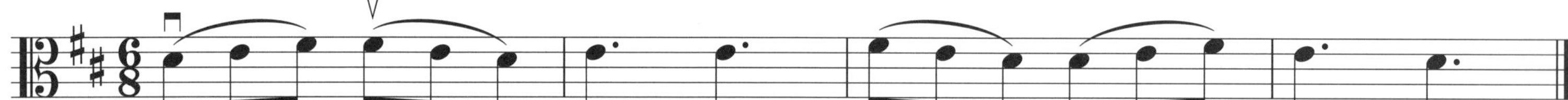

120. JOLLY GOOD FELLOW

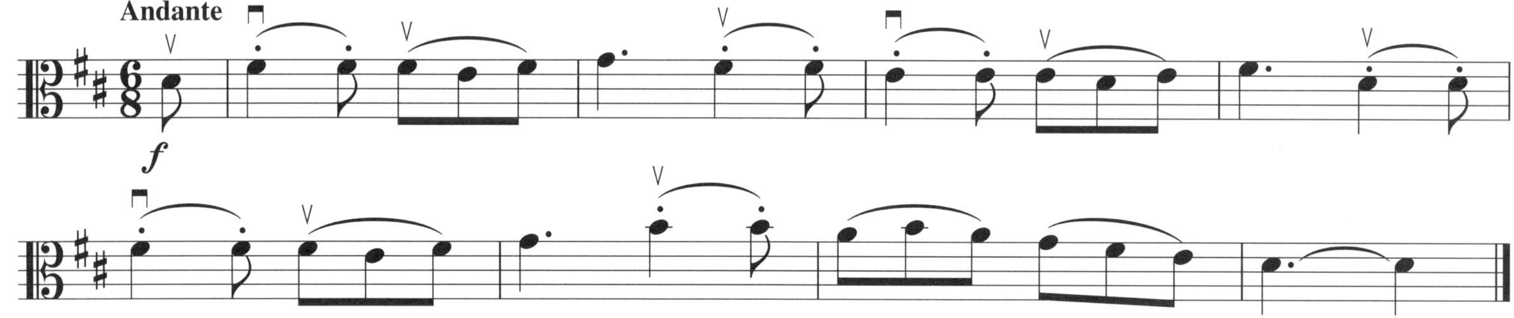

$\frac{6}{8}$ Time Signature

When music in $\frac{6}{8}$ time is played fast, it is easier to stress beats one and four, and "feel" the pulse in two large beats.

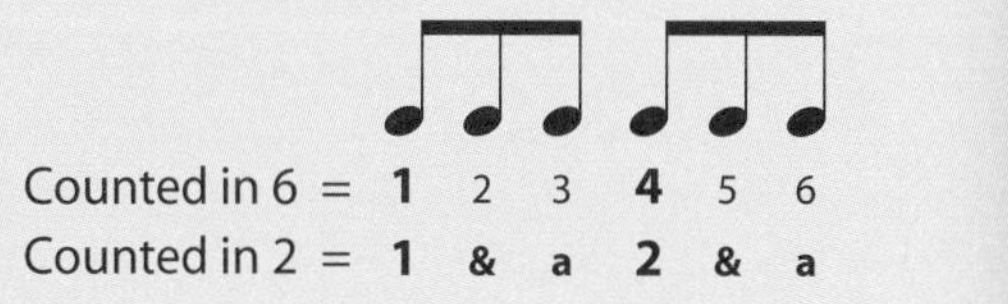

THEORY

121. RHYTHM RAP

Shadow bow and count before playing.

6/8 RHYTHMS

122. RISE AND FALL

123. BEACH WALK

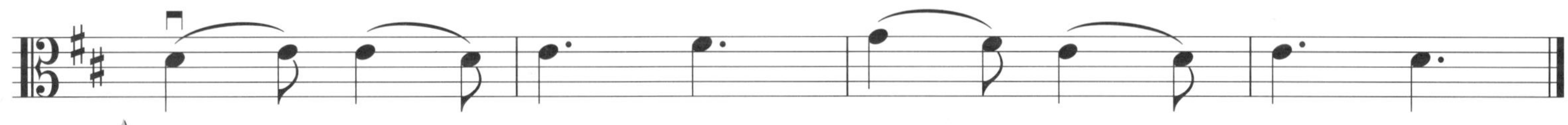

Write in the correct time signature before you begin.

Austrian composer **Wolfgang Amadeus Mozart** was a child prodigy who lived during the American Revolution. At five, he was composing music, and by his early teens he had mastered the violin. Mozart wrote more than 600 compositions during his short life, including oratorios, symphonies, concertos, and operas. Imagine and describe the career of a composer.

HISTORY

124. MAY TIME

W. A. Mozart (1756–1791)

THEORY

Minor Scales

A minor scale is a series of eight notes which follow a definite pattern of whole steps and half steps. There are three forms of the minor scale; natural minor, harmonic minor, and melodic minor. The D minor (natural) scale uses the same pitches as the F major scale.

125. D MINOR (Natural) SCALE

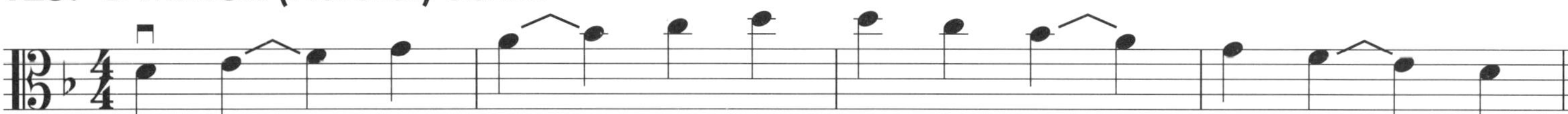

HISTORY

Austrian composer **Gustav Mahler** was also a successful conductor. He believed in unifying the arts and often combined music, poetry, and philosophy in his compositions. Exercise 126 *Mahler's Theme* first appears in his *Symphony No. 1,* played as a solo by the double bass. During Mahler's lifetime Vincent van Gogh created his most famous paintings, and Mark Twain wrote *Tom Sawyer.*

126. MAHLER'S THEME – Round

Gustav Mahler (1860–1911)

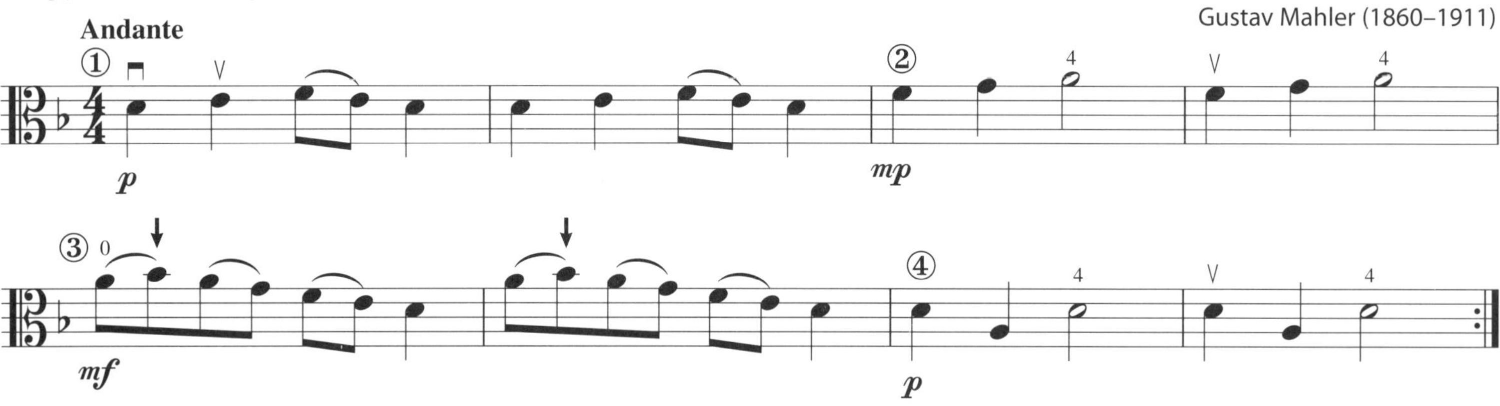

127. SHALOM CHAVERIM – Round

Hebrew Folk Song

128. THE SNAKE CHARMER

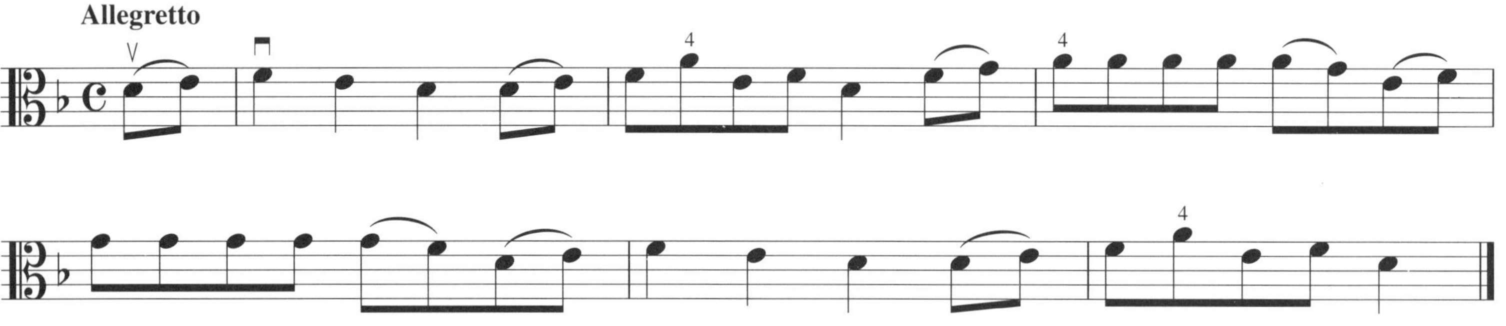

Key Signature
G MINOR

THEORY

The G minor (natural) scale uses the same pitches as the B♭ major scale.

129. G MINOR (Natural) SCALE

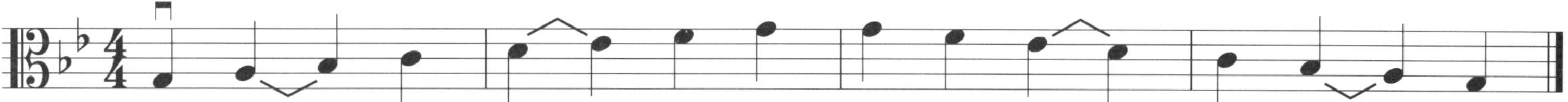

HISTORY

With the establishment of Israel as an independent political state in 1948, *Hatikvah* became the Israeli National Anthem. The same year Mohandas Gandhi was assassinated in India. Israeli violinists Itzhak Perlman and Pinchas Zukerman are concert artists known throughout the world.

130. HATIKVAH

131. G MINOR (Natural) SCALE *(Upper Octave – violin)*

132. ESSENTIAL ELEMENTS QUIZ – THE HANUKKAH SONG

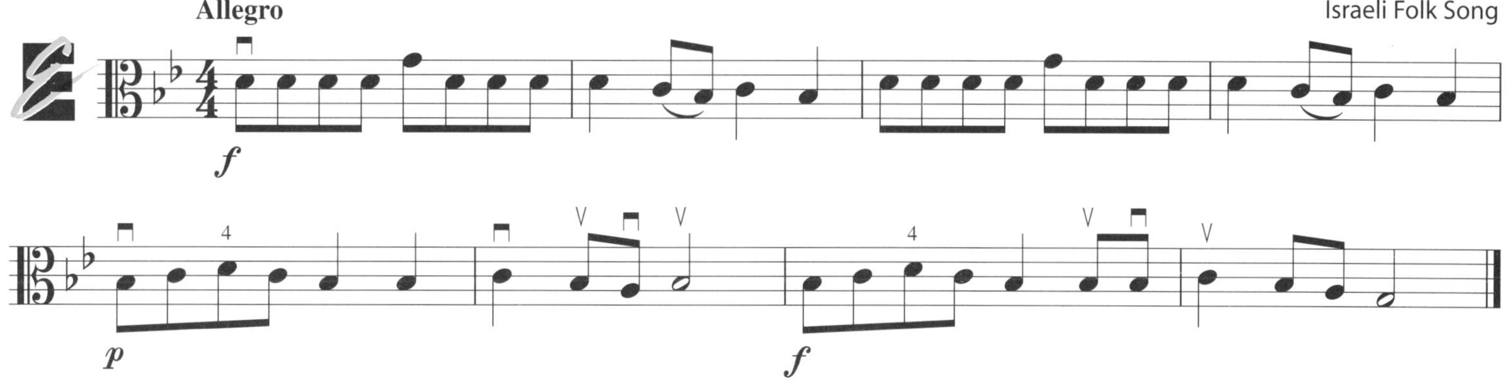

THEORY

Mixed Meter

Occasionally the meter (time signature) changes in music. Watch for meter changes and count carefully.

MIXED METER

133. RHYTHM RAP

Shadow bow and count before playing.

134. FRENCH FOLK SONG

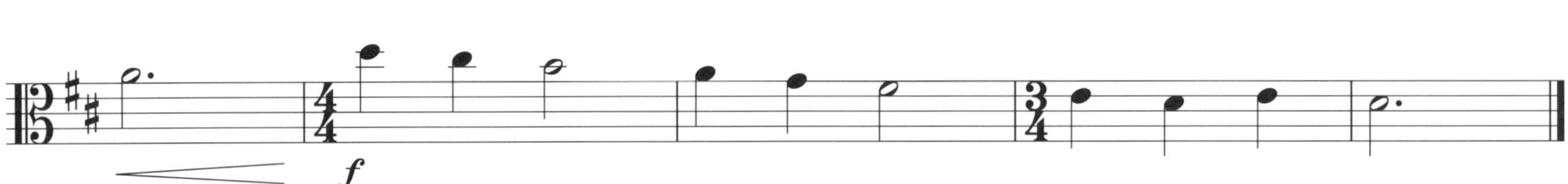

Cantabile

In a singing style.

e The Italian word for "and."

135. KUM BA YAH

African Spiritual

A **triplet** is a group of three notes. In $\frac{2}{4}$, $\frac{3}{4}$, or $\frac{4}{4}$ time, an eighth note triplet is spread evenly across one beat.

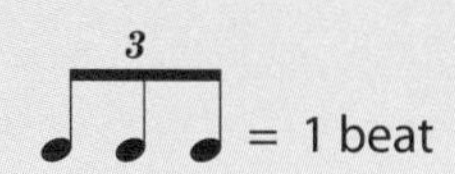

THEORY

RHYTHMS

136. RHYTHM RAP

Shadow bow and count before playing.

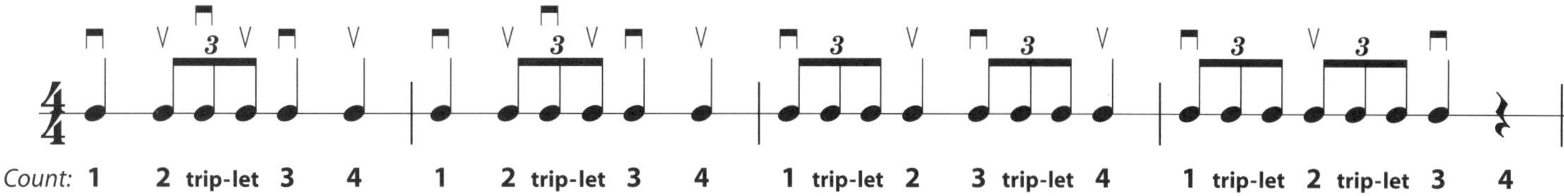

137. D MAJOR SCALE WITH TRIPLETS

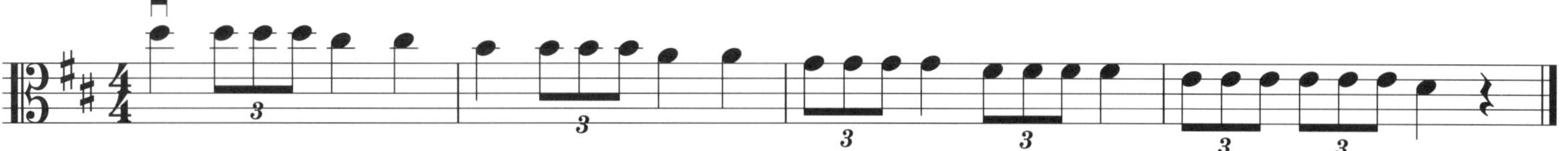

138. ON THE MOVE

139. SLURRING TRIPLETS

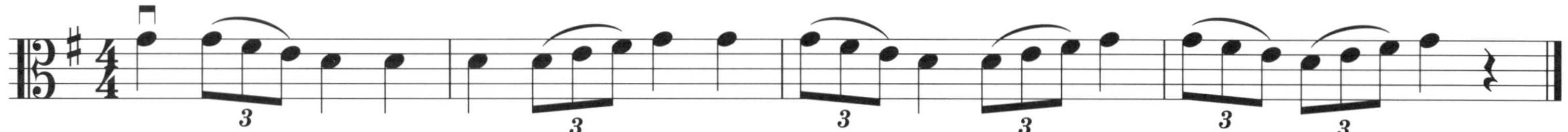

140. TRIPLET ETUDE

141. LITTLE RIVER

142. FIELD SONG

Southern American Folk Song

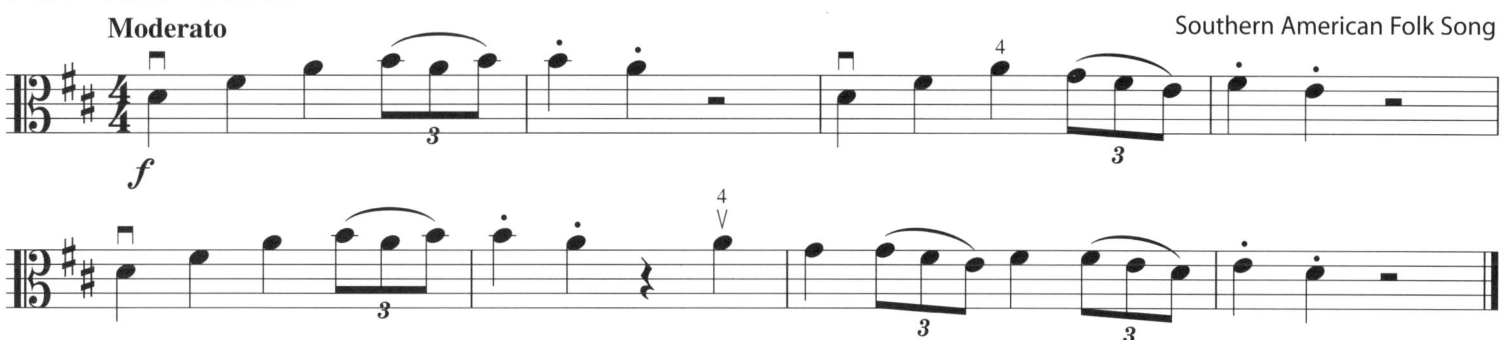

THEORY

¢ Time Signature Cut Time (Alla Breve)

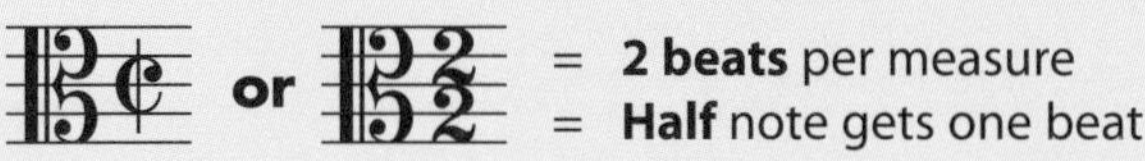

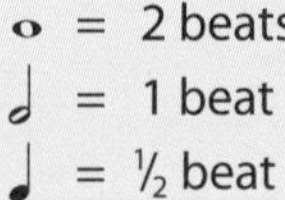

143. RHYTHM RAP

Shadow bow and count before playing.

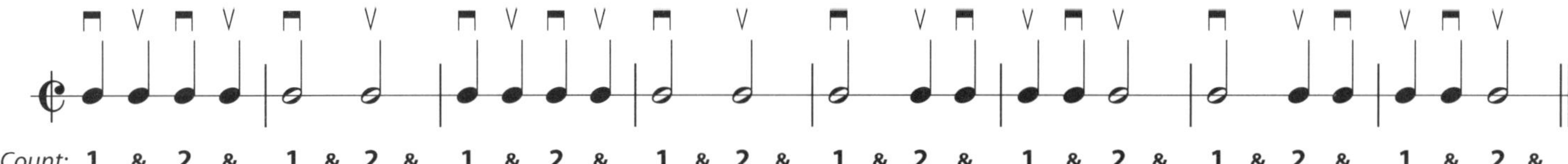

144. A CUT ABOVE

145. CUT TIME MARCH

146. RHYTHM RAP

Shadow bow and count before playing.

147. SYNCOPATION MARCH

148. WHEN THE SAINTS GO MARCHIN' IN

Allegro

James M. Black

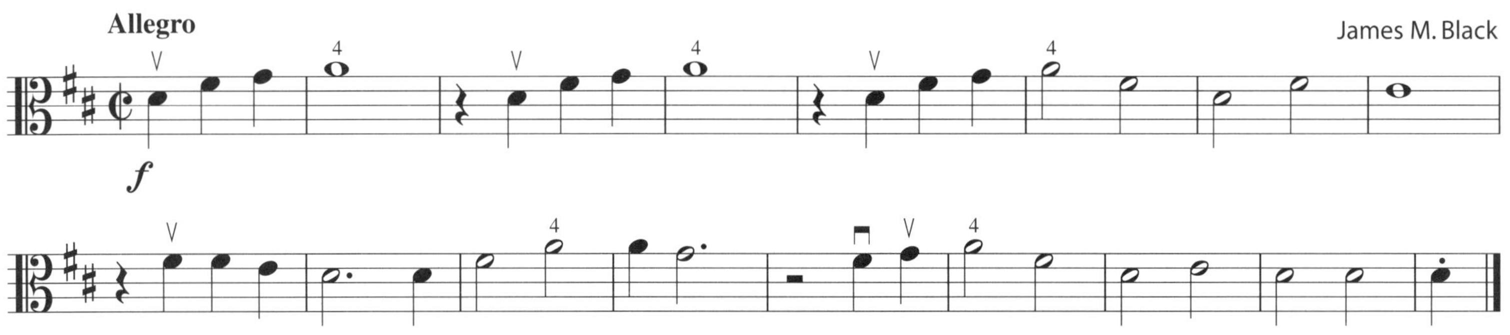

✓ Are you counting in cut time?

149. RHYTHM RAP

Shadow bow and count before playing.

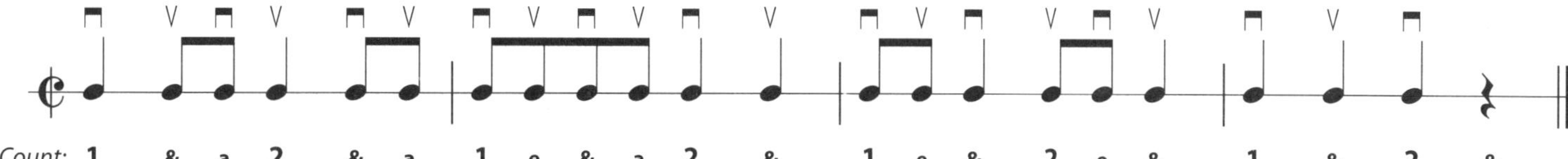

150. DOWN HOME

151. MOVING ALONG

152. RHYTHM RAP

Shadow bow and count before playing.

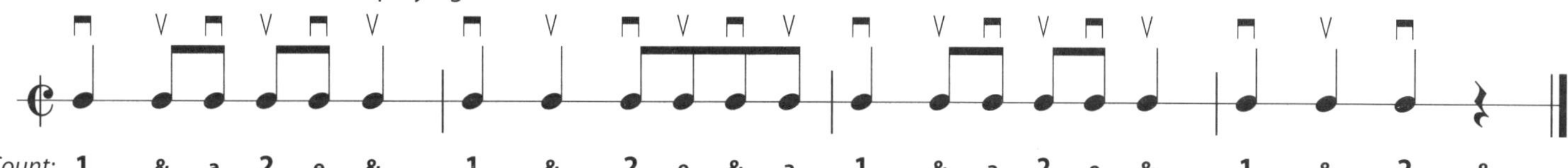

153. UP TOWN

154. FLYING BOWS

C RHYTHMS

HISTORY

Cantatas are pieces much like short operas that were written during the **Baroque Period** (1600–1750). They involve vocal soloists and choirs that are accompanied by small orchestras. **Johann Sebastian Bach** wrote nearly 300 of them between 1704 and 1745. While Bach was composing his cantatas, the famous philosopher Voltaire was writing his books and Thomas Jefferson, the great United States president, was born.

155. MARCH FROM PEASANT'S CANTATA

Allegretto J. S. Bach (1685–1750)

PERFORMANCE SPOTLIGHT

Performing music for others is fun and rewarding. Either small or large ensembles can perform the following arrangements. Always observe proper concert etiquette by being well prepared, dressing appropriately, being on time, and remembering all equipment. Show respect when others are playing by listening attentively and applauding at the appropriate time.

156. SAGEBRUSH OVERTURE – Orchestra Arrangement A = Melody part. B = Orchestra part.

✓ What were the strong points of your performance?

157. POMP AND CIRCUMSTANCE – Orchestra Arrangement
Moderato
A = Melody part. B = Orchestra part.
Edward Elgar (1857–1933)
Arr. John Higgins
A
B
mp - f
1.
2.
11
rit.
158. AMERICA THE BEAUTIFUL – Orchestra Arrangement
Andante e legato
A = Melody part. B = Orchestra part.
Samuel Augustus Ward (1847–1903)
Arr. John Higgins
mp
mf
9
f
PERFORMANCE SPOTLIGHT

159. LA BAMBA – Duet

Mexican Folk Song
Arr. Michael Allen

Allegro

A
B

f

Fine

D.C. al Fine

p

PERFORMANCE SPOTLIGHT

HISTORY

Gustav Holst was a famous British orchestra composer who frequently set words to music, including poems by the American poet, Walt Whitman. Holst's *St. Paul's Suite* for string orchestra was written for the St. Paul's Girls School Orchestra and published in 1913. His best known work is *The Planets,* first performed in 1918, the same year as the end of World War I.

160. IN THE BLEAK MIDWINTER – Orchestra Arrangement

Gustav Holst (1874–1934)
Arr. John Higgins

Andante

A = Melody part. **B** = Orchestra part.

A
B

mp

9

mf

13

mp

rit.

p

161. SWALLOWTAIL JIG – Orchestra Arrangement

A = Melody part. **B** = Orchestra part.

Irish Jig
Arr. John Higgins

Sight-reading

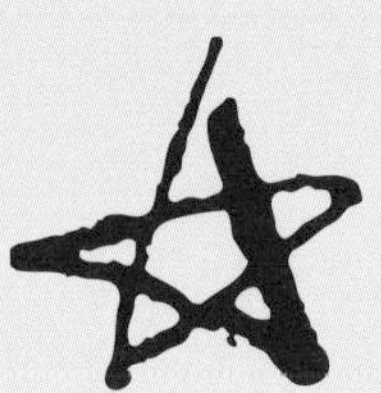

Sight-reading means playing a musical piece for the first time. The key to sight-reading success is to know what to look for *before* you play. Use the word **S-T-A-R-S** to remind yourself what to look for, and eventually your orchestra will become sight-reading STARS!

S — **Sharps or flats** in the key signature
T — **Time signature** and **tempo markings**
A — **Accidentals** not found in the key signature
R — **Rhythms**, silently counting the more difficult notes and rests
S — **Signs**, including dynamics, articulations, repeats and endings

162. SIGHT-READING CHALLENGE #1

163. SIGHT-READING CHALLENGE #2

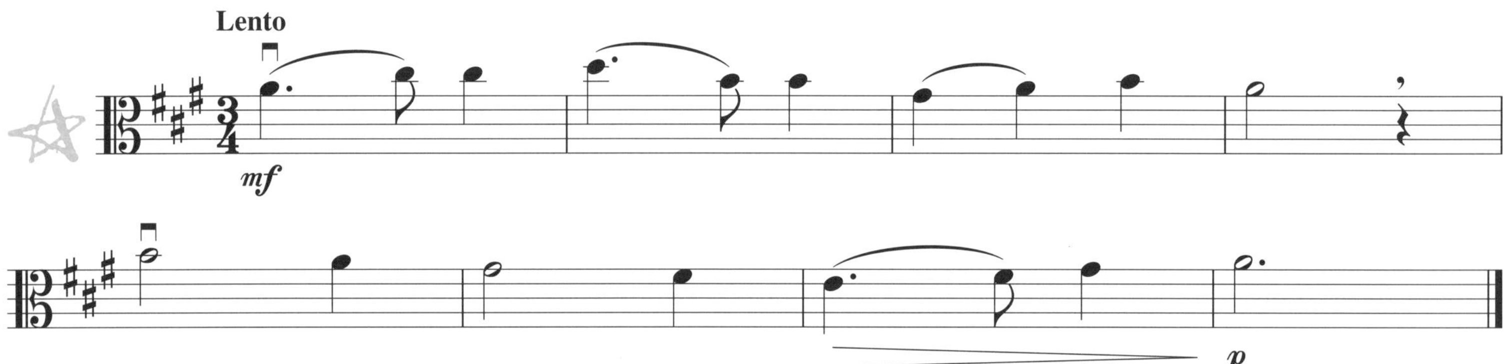

164. SIGHT-READING CHALLENGE #3

165. SIGHT-READING CHALLENGE #4

Natural Harmonic

Natural harmonics are tones created by a vibrating string divided into equal sections. To play an octave higher than an open string, lightly touch the string exactly half way between the bridge and the nut. In the following examples, harmonics are indicated by a "○" above a note, plus a fingering number. $\overset{4}{\circ}$ indicates a harmonic played with the fourth finger.

Shifting

Sliding your left hand smoothly and lightly to a new location on the fingerboard, indicated by a dash (–). Be sure your thumb moves with your hand.

FINGER PATTERNS

There are four basic finger patterns, which are combinations of whole and half steps. In the "open" hand pattern, a half step occurs between the open string and first finger. The other patterns have half steps between 1–2, 2–3, or 3–4. Notice that some finger patterns include new notes.

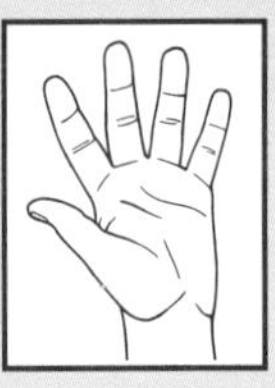
open hand

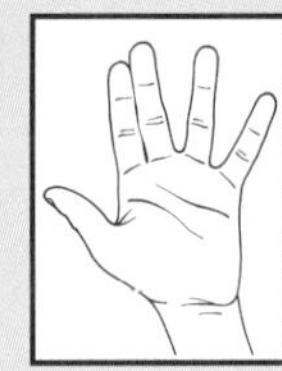
1–2

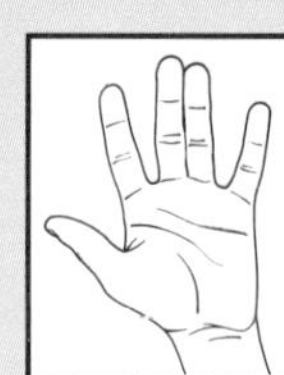
2–3

3–4

FINGER PATTERNS (By Pattern)

174. 3–4 PATTERN

175. 2–3 PATTERN

176. 1–2 PATTERN

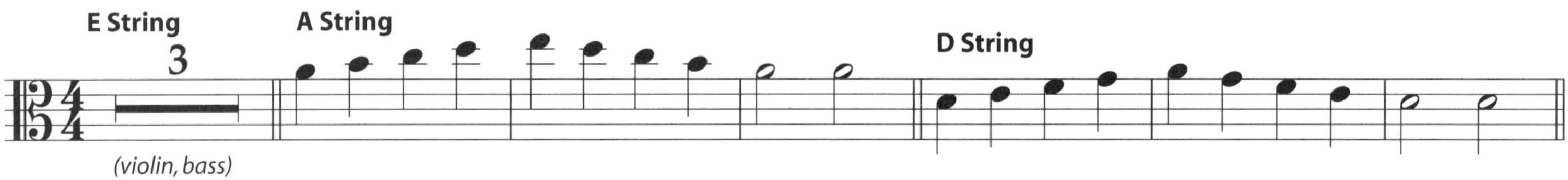

177. OPEN PATTERN

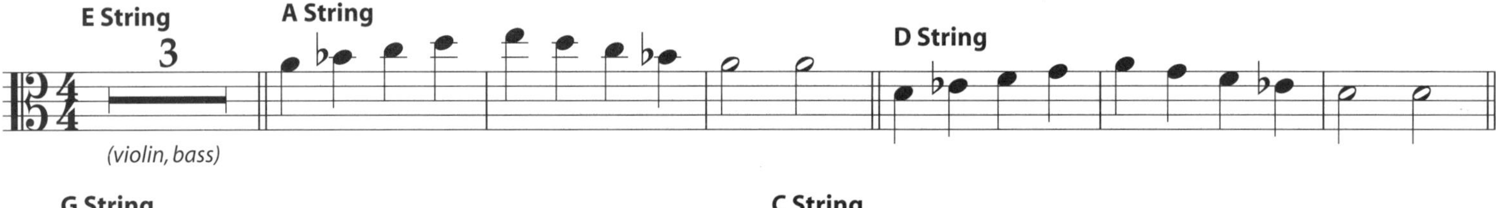

FINGER PATTERNS (By String)

FINGER PATTERNS (By Key)

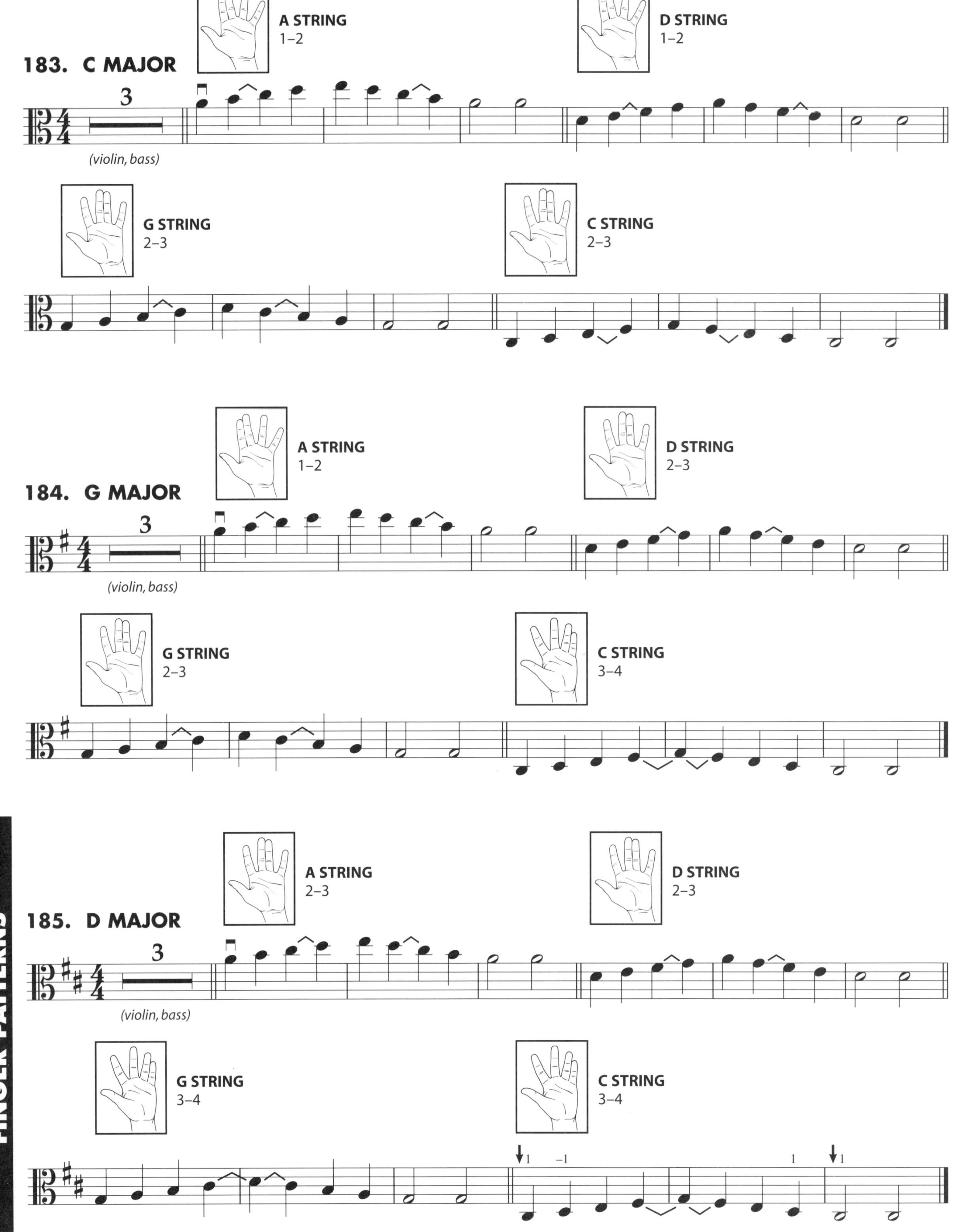

186. A MAJOR

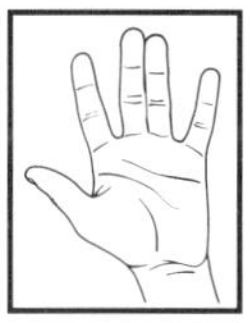

A STRING
2–3

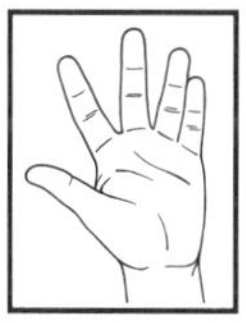

D STRING
3–4

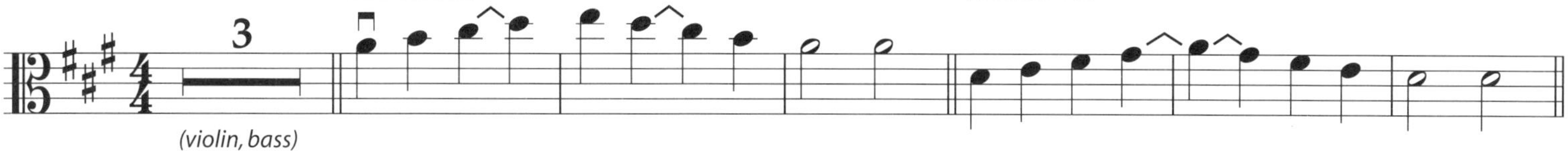

3

(violin, bass)

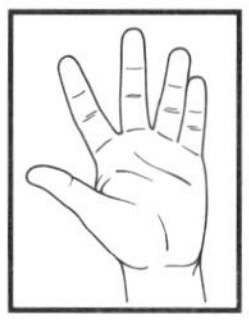

G STRING
3–4

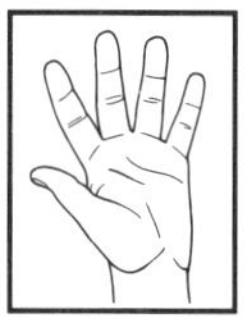

C STRING
open hand

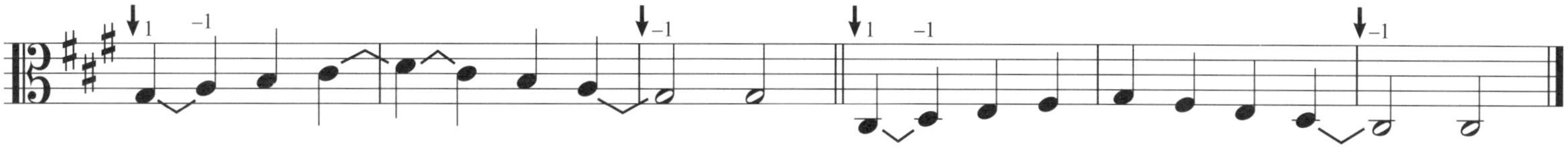

1 –1 –1 1 –1 –1

187. F MAJOR

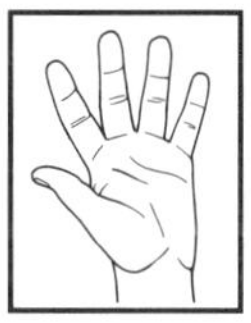

A STRING
open hand

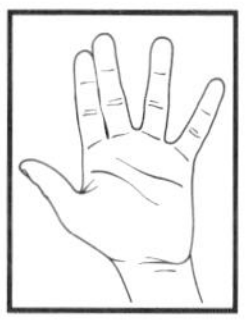

D STRING
1–2

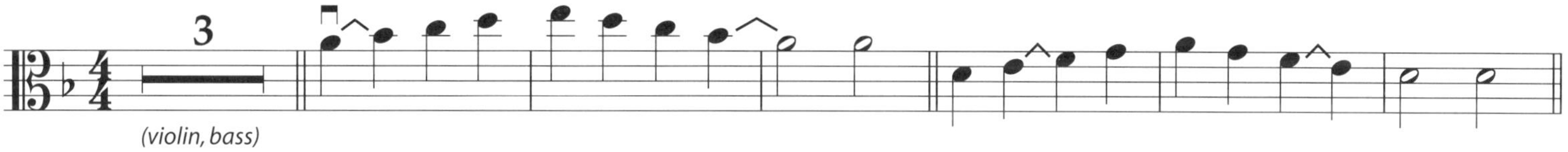

3

(violin, bass)

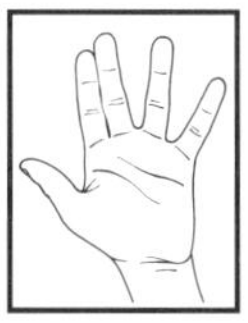

G STRING
1–2

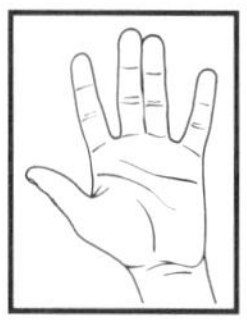

C STRING
2–3

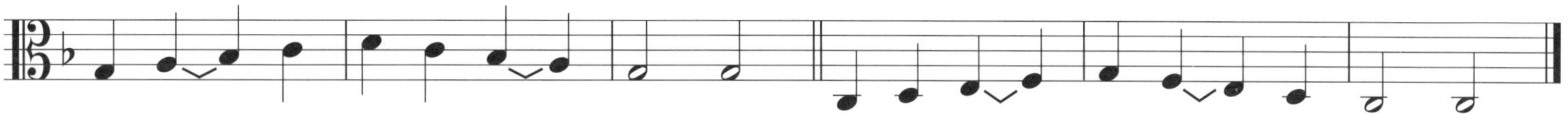

188. B♭ MAJOR

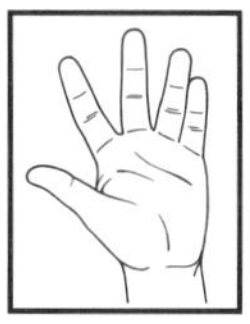

A STRING
3–4

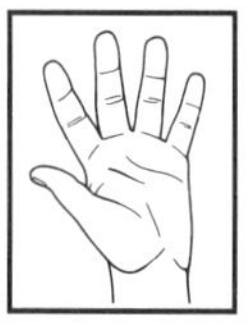

D STRING
open hand

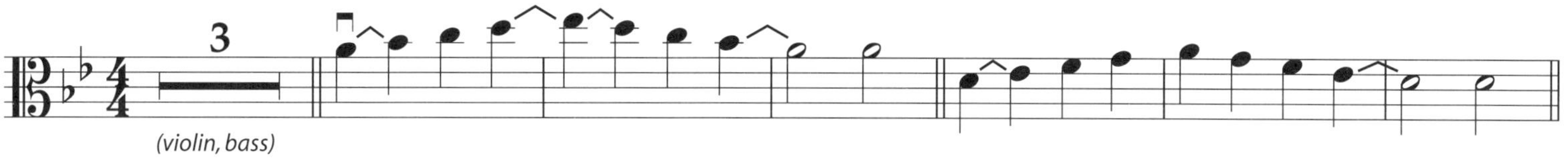

3

(violin, bass)

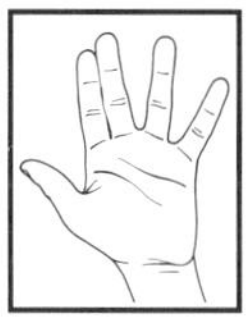

G STRING
1–2

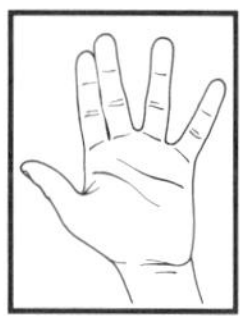

C STRING
1–2

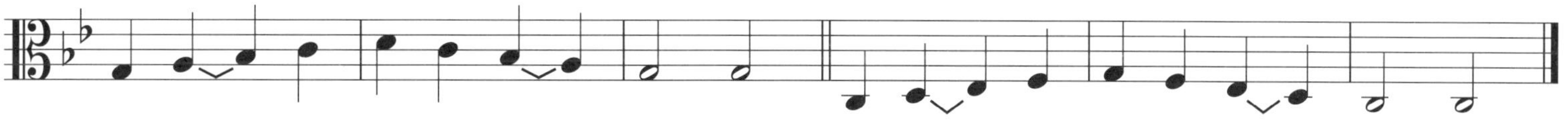

SCALES AND ARPEGGIOS

Identify two important elements of performing scales and arpeggios accurately.
As you play each line, check to make sure you are able to do these things.

189. C MAJOR

190. C MAJOR

191. G MAJOR

192. G MAJOR *(Upper Octave – violin)*

193. D MAJOR

194. D MAJOR

195. A MAJOR

196. A MAJOR *(Upper Octave – violin)*

197. F MAJOR

198. B♭ MAJOR

199. B♭ MAJOR *(Upper Octave – violin)*

200. D MINOR (Natural)

201. D MINOR (Natural)

202. G MINOR (Natural)

203. G MINOR (Natural) *(Upper Octave – violin)*

CREATING MUSIC

THEORY

Improvisation

Improvisation is the art of freely creating your own music as you play.

204. *Using the following notes, improvise your own melody (Line A) to go with the accompaniment (Line B).*

THEORY

Composition

Composition is the art of writing original music. A composer often begins by creating a melody made up of individual **phrases**, like short musical "sentences." Some melodies have phrases that seem to answer or respond to "question" phrases, as in Beethoven's *Ode To Joy.* Play this melody and listen to how phrase 2 answers phrase 1.

205. ODE TO JOY

Ludwig van Beethoven (1770–1827)

206. PHRASE BUILDERS *Write 2 different phrases using the following rhythms.*

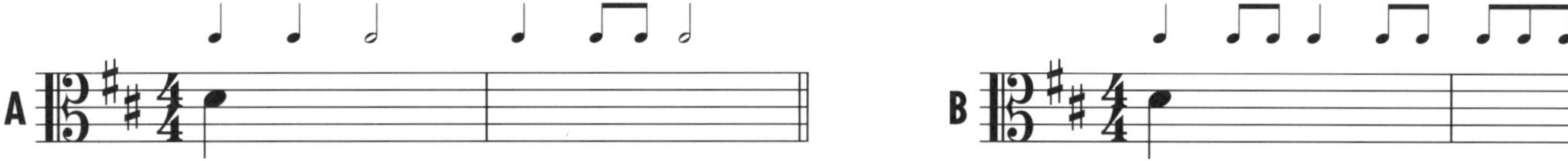

207. Q. AND A. *Write your own "answer" to the following melodies.*

208. YOU NAME IT: ______________________________ *Now write your own music.*

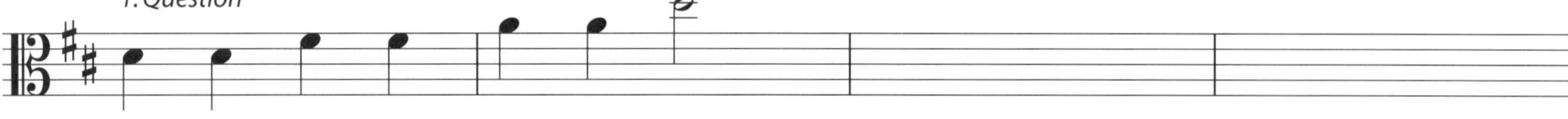

IMPROVISATION/COMPOSITION

Double Stops

A **double stop** is playing two strings at once.

209. TWO AT A TIME

210. ADDING FINGERS

VIOLA FINGERING CHART

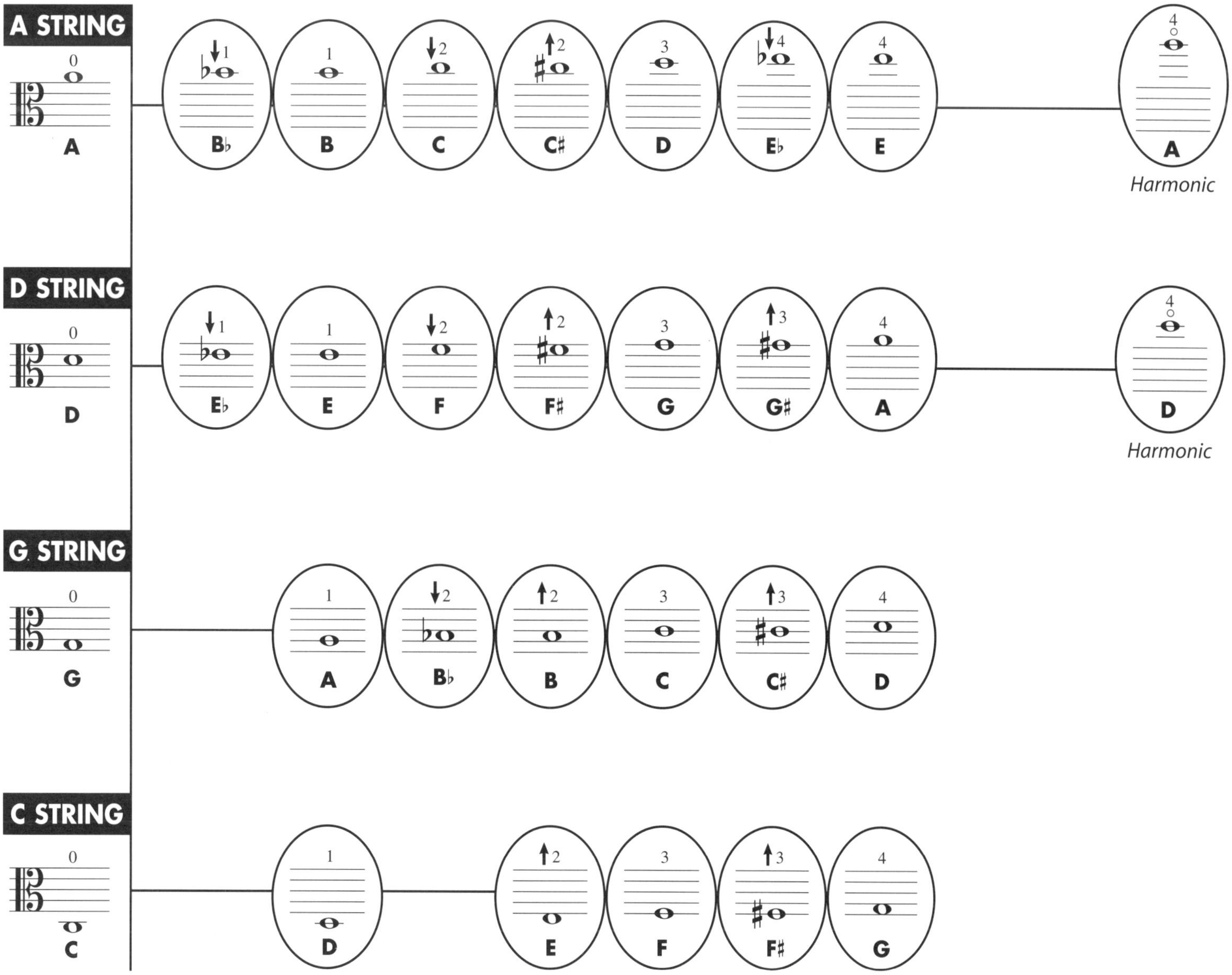

String	Open (0)								
A STRING	0 A	↓1 B♭	1 B	↓2 C	↑2 C♯	3 D	↓4 E♭	4 E	4 (o) A *Harmonic*
D STRING	0 D	↓1 E♭	1 E	↓2 F	↑2 F♯	3 G	↑3 G♯	4 A	4 (o) D *Harmonic*
G STRING	0 G		1 A	↓2 B♭	↑2 B	3 C	↑3 C♯	4 D	
C STRING	0 C		1 D		↑2 E	3 F	↑3 F♯	4 G	

REFERENCE INDEX

Definitions (pg.)

Book I Review

Composers

World Music